Marketing Information and Research 2008-2009

Marketing Information and Research 2008–2009

Matthew Housden

AMSTERDAM • BOSTON • HEIDELBERG • LONDON • NEW YORK • OXFORD
PARIS • SAN DIEGO • SAN FRANCISCO • SINGAPORE • SYDNEY • TOKYO

Butterworth-Heinemann is an imprint of Elsevier

Butterworth-Heinemann is an imprint of Elsevier
Linacre House, Jordan Hill, Oxford OX2 8DP, UK
30 Corporate Drive, Suite 400, Burlington, MA 01803, USA

First edition 2008
Copyright 2008 Elsevier Ltd. All rights reserved

Notice
No responsibility is assumed by the publisher for any injury and/or damage to persons
or property as a matter of products liability, negligence or otherwise, or from any use
or operation of any methods, products, instructions or ideas contained in the material
herein.

British Library Cataloguing in Publication Data
A catalogue record for this book is available from the British Library.

Library of Congress Cataloguing in Publication Data
A catalogue record for this book is available from the Library of Congress.

ISBN: 978 0 7506 8964 9

For information on all Butterworth-Heinemann publications
visit our website at http://www.elsevierdirect.com

 Designed and typeset by P.K. McBride

Printed and bound in Italy
08   09   10   11   12   10 9 8 7 6 5 4 3 2 1

Contents

Unit 1
The role of information in marketing

Learning objectives

By the end of this unit you will be able to:

◆ Discuss the need for information in marketing management and its role in the overall marketing process.

◆ Identify the role of information on customers.

◆ Identify the need for and scope of information on competitors and stakeholders.

◆ Understand the nature of the marketing environment and PEST research.

◆ Understand the nature of marketing information and its role in describing, comparing and diagnosing marketing problems.

◆ Evaluate the impact of information technology on the marketing function and discuss the challenges facing organizations in collecting valid, reliable and measurable information to support the decision-making process.

◆ Identify the growth in information sources.

◆ Identify the role of the Internet, intranets and extranets.

◆ Understand the role of online communities, discussion boards and blogs.

◆ Describe the nature of customer databases and other decision support systems.

◆ Evaluate the variability and reliability of information sources.

Table 1.1: Learning outcomes and knowledge and skills requirements

Learning outcomes	Knowledge and skills requirements
1.1 Identify appropriate information and marketing research requirements for marketing decision-making.	Discuss the need for information in marketing management and its role in the overall marketing process
	Information on customers
	Information on competitors and other organizations
	Information on the marketing environment
	Descriptive v. comparative v. diagnostic role
1.2 Evaluate the impact of information technology on the marketing function and discuss the challenges facing organizations in collecting valid, reliable and measurable information to support the decision making process	Growth in information sources (the information explosion)
	The Internet/intranets
	On-line communities/blogs

Key definitions

Marketing – Marketing is the management process responsible for identifying, anticipating and satisfying customer requirements profitably. (CIM, 2007)

Internet –A global computing network

Extranet – A group of websites that combine to share data and information. Access is limited to authorized users

Intranet – An in-house website that serves the employees or members of an organizations or authorized users

Marketing research – The collection, analysis and communication of information undertaken to assist decision-making in marketing. (Wilson, 2006)

The marketing database – A manual or computerized source of data relevant to marketing decision-making about an organization's customers. (Wilson, 2006)

Study guide

This unit should take you around two hours to complete. You should supplement your reading of the unit with at least two hours' activity around the unit including reading relevant sections of the recommended texts and reviewing the trade press to begin your case study and clippings portfolio.

Introduction

As the Industrial Revolution took hold in the 18th and 19th centuries, the ports of the world were full of ships loading and unloading goods from all around the globe. The industry that insured much the risk associated with this trade was based in Edward Lloyd's coffee house in Tower Street in London, first mentioned in February 1689 in the *London Gazette*. The exchanges, as they became known, essentially exchanged information. Customers of Lloyd would exchange gossip, rumour and evidence on shipping, ports and even acts of piracy. This would enable them to evaluate and assess the level of risk which would affect their investments.

Today many of those ports lie empty and the physical trade in goods is focused around the great transportation hubs of, for example, Singapore and Memphis. Lloyds remains and still insures much of the risks involved. In 2008 the capacity of Lloyds was £15.95 billion, (Lloyds 2008).

The information that drives this market is now exchanged at the touch of a button and this means that Lloyds' names could if they wished, run their businesses from the modern coffee houses, Starbucks or Monmouth Coffee Company for example, via mobile or other wireless networks. They might even access Lloyds List online at www.lloydslist.com, a legacy of Edward Lloyd and still providing the sector with pertinent, reliable, accurate and timely information today.

Marketing and information

Peter Chisnall in his 2004 book, *Marketing Research*, calls information the raw material of management. Without information we cannot make informed decisions. There will always be risk attached to business decisions but good information will help us measure, manage and assess the degree of risk involved in making business and marketing decisions.

What is marketing?

By now you should know the CIM definition of marketing.

Activity 1.1

Write down the CIM definition of marketing. If you can't remember it go to the CIM website. www.cim.co.uk.

There has been debate about a new definition of marketing and the CIM have proposed the following change. The new definition which has been under consideration is:

> *The strategic business function that creates value by stimulating, facilitating and fulfilling customer demand. It does this by building brands, nurturing innovation, developing relationships, creating good customer service and communicating benefits. By operating customer-centrically, marketing brings positive return on investment, satisfies shareholders and stake-holders from business and the community, and contributes to positive behavioural change and a sustainable business future.*

Other definitions

The American Marketing Association (www.marketingpower.com) defines marketing slightly differently as:

> *an organizational function and a set of processes for creating, communicating and delivering value to customers and for managing customer relationships in ways that benefit the organization and its stakeholders.*

The Marketing Society (www.marketing-society.org.uk) defines it even more simply:

> *The creation of customer demand, which is the only sustainable form of growth in business.*

Give that this course is about the role of information and research in marketing it would be useful to think about what required information is indicated within the definitions.

Let us have a look at the CIM definition in detail.

Marketing is a management process

We will not dwell too long on this. It is enough to say that marketing is about getting things done through and with people. We need to work with a range of colleagues, suppliers and intermediaries to deliver satisfaction to our customers.

'Customers' is an interesting word. They are the only reason businesses exist. It is easy to say marketing is about customers but even this simple word has multiple meaning in the marketing context. Are we talking about current customers, lapsed customers, future customers, profitable customers, best customers or key account customers? The list is as long as the number of segmentation variables we can use.

Of equal interest to us are the next few words.

Marketing is about identifying customer needs

This sounds straightforward. Let us think about this in more detail.

Activity 1.2

I buy mineral water. What need am I fulfilling? Write down as many as you can think of. It may help you to think about the context in which a person may buy water. Think hard, you should have at least six points.

You can see that there are a range of needs that are being satisfied. They depend on the type of person, their financial background, their age, their household composition, their life style, whether they are buying for a business or to resell.

The basic need, that is 'I'm thirsty', is the simplest to understand. The more complex needs emerge from a greater understanding of the way a product or service is consumed. This is the role of research and information.

The anticipation of customer needs

This task is even harder. Forecasting has been described as trying to tell someone where to steer a car by looking through the rear window. Think about the pace of development of new technology. Gordon Moore of Intel Corporation, the computer chip manufacturer, has said that the processing power of computers will double every 18 months and the price will halve. This has become known as Moore's Law. He was right and wrong. The pace of change has been faster. Those companies that are at the forefront of the IT revolution have found it very hard to anticipate customer needs as the customers themselves have found it hard to understand the pace of change and how this might affect their buying patterns.

The IT revolution and the airlines

In the mid-1990s, airlines were re-specifying their fleets. The lead-time for commissioning and delivery of new planes is significant. Airlines asked their business customers what changes they would like to see. Some said more legroom, some said better food and more choice of films. Some said that they would like to telephone from the plane. Only a few mentioned at-seat power jacks for their laptops. This meant that many of the new planes that came on line in the late 1990s and early 2000s did not allow business executives to run laptops other than on the laptop's battery.

It is not always enough simply to ask your customers what they want. The questions have to be asked in the right way. We will look at this in detail later on.

Some markets change quickly, others evolve but they always change. As Hugh Davidson (1997) says 'tomorrow's standards are always higher'. The information strategy of the organization must be set up to ensure that these changes can be anticipated, monitored and acted upon. Risk can never be eliminated from business decision-making. The key thing is to manage and, where possible, reduce the levels of risk to which the organization is subject to within acceptable levels relative to required return on shareholders' investments.

Customer satisfaction

This has been an area of growth in marketing over the last 10 years as concepts of relationship marketing and Customer Relationship Management (CRM) have become popularized and applied in businesses.

The measurement of lifetime value and work on loyalty (notably by Frederick Reichheld (2001) in his book *The Loyalty Effect*) has shifted the emphasis from one of sales and new business to customer retention and repeat business. A corollary of this has been a focus on customer satisfaction. The idea is that satisfied customers stay loyal, and loyal customers are more profitable. Well again, research shows that this is not always the case. Customers may be satisfied but still leave. They may be enticed away by better offers or products or may no longer have a need for our products or services. They may seek variety or new experiences. Jones and Sasser's (1995) article in the Harvard Business Review confirms that satisfied customers do defect.

So establishing levels of satisfaction is not enough. The organization must ensure that the underlying attitudes and behaviours are revealed. If customers do defect, then the organization needs to ensure that the reasons for leaving are established and changes are made if appropriate.

Profit

The reason we are in business. Simple? Well not really. The development of the marketing database that captures data on the buying behaviour of customers means that we can begin to see that some customers are more profitable than others.

We can see that the Pareto Effect which states that 20 per cent of customers account for around 80 per cent of profit is generally true. Indeed in many businesses less than 20 per cent of customers account for more than 80 per cent of profits. Kraft recently discovered that 20 per cent of customers accounted for 105 per cent of profits. This means that 80 per cent of customers are losing them money. So if under Henry Ford all customers were created equal, we now can prove that some customers are more equal than others.

P&O and Elsie Mader

P&O ran a competition to establish who had been on P&O cruises the longest. The winner was Elsie Mader. She had been cruising with P&O so many times that her total time aboard came to more than 10 years.

Source: IDM Course Material.

Companies are using this information to work out which customers they need to retain, and by profiling existing highly profitable customers they can more easily identify the type of customer they wish to recruit. For P&O this would be more Elsie Maders! More controversially some companies are using this transactional data to deselect or 'sack' customers who are unprofitable.

Another aspect of profit is deciding when to take profit. Companies using direct response techniques know that many customers are acquired at a loss. The relationship with customers only makes sense from a business perspective over time.

Insight: Direct insurance

The average cost of acquiring a customer in the insurance market has been estimated as £120. If the premium is £200, it is clear that this does not allow for very much profit to be made on a one-off transaction. This is why as soon as you buy insurance products you will receive mailings for extended cover, other insurance products or other financial services products.

So the definition of marketing is not as straightforward as perhaps it first appeared. At the centre of all the elements of the definition is the need for information and research, analysis and insight that allow for a depth of understanding and marketing decisions made at reduced risk.

The role of customer information

Let's look at the definitions one more time:

The consistent element of all definitions is customers:

◆ We need to be able to identify customers

◆ We need to stimulate their demand

◆ We need to be able to identify and understand their needs

◆ We need to be able to anticipate their needs into the future

◆ We need to communicate with them

◆ We need to manage relationships with them, which implies continuity

◆ We may need to change their behaviour

◆ We need to create value for them and for us. In most cases this means make profits from them.

So it is clear that information on customers should be at the heart of any information and research strategy. However there are a range of other factors that will prevent us from dealing with 'customers profitably'.

Information on competitors and other stakeholders

Customer information is not all that is needed. There are a number of organizations that impact on our ability to do business. They range from those who are active in helping to deliver value to those who have an interest in the way we do business.

> **Stakeholders** – those individuals or groups who depend on the organization to fulfil their own goals and on whom the organization depends. (Johnson, *et al.* 2008)

Activity 1.3

For your own organization or an organization of your choice outline the range of stakeholder that exert an influence on the business. What information would you want to know about them? Think briefly about how you might obtain this.

Clearly profits come from customers but future profits may come from other companies' customers. The competition is also trying to make profits from customers and we are all going after the same markets.

In a time of low growth, future profits may come from share steal and we need to understand the point of difference of our competitors and try to predict their future actions. The need for a competitor intelligence system is important.

Wilson (2006) in the core text suggests a system needs to :

◆ Identify the key competitors

◆ Allocate resources

◆ Select and brief data collectors

◆ Insist on regular returns

◆ Publish regular reports.

Equally important is the role of suppliers and intermediaries in creating value for our customers. Intermediaries, for example wholesalers or retailers or the sales force, play a vital role in the way our brand is received. We need information on these influencers on our customers.

Finally there are a range of other stakeholders who have an influence on our ability to deliver satisfaction. For example unions may work positively or negatively on our behalf a range of pressure groups may monitor activities, for example, environmental groups.

The nature of the marketing environment and PEST research

As well as the organizations that influence our ability to market we work within a dynamic marketing environment. No business exists in a vacuum. Organizations interact and engage with and to some extent, influence the environment within which they exist. The environment is the source of business opportunities and the resources that we have at our disposal to exploit these opportunities. Of course it is also a source of threat. We have discussed the fact that competitors are looking to steal our customers and outperform us in other key areas.

New technology may make our products obsolete almost overnight. In utilities or financial services, industries that are constantly scrutinized and heavily regulated, new rules on tax or legislation relating to lending and credit may impact significantly on organizations' profitability or ability to compete.

The environment then is an essential factor in the development of marketing strategy. Rosbeth Moss Kanter describes this as 'dancing on a moving carpet' (Kanter 1984). Within the analogy of the fairground ride lies the uncertainty that is present in every organization, and the difficulty of predicting and managing this.

The PESTEL model

Within marketing we generally classify the environment under the headings:

◆ Political

◆ Economic

◆ Social

◆ Technological

◆ Environmental (or green) issues

◆ Legal.

The PESTEL framework is simple shorthand for those factors that impact on the ability of the organization to achieve its strategic objectives but which lay outside the organization's direct control.

You may also see this written in the following ways:

◆ PEST

◆ STEP

◆ SLEPT adds the legal dimension

◆ PLESTIE adds 'I', Industry factors and 'E', Ethical issues

◆ PLESTIE + C adds 'C', Competitive factors

Activity 1.4

For each of the factors within the PESTEL framework outline the range of information that may be required.

Marketing planning and the role of information

The average salary of the typical marketing director is around £80,000 plus benefits, he (typically it is still a he) reads the broadsheets and *Marketing* or *Marketing Week*. He goes on two holidays a year with his family and likes to watch *The Apprentice*.

The average household income in the UK is around £23,000. Typically we like to read *The Sun*, we try to take a holiday and we do like *The Apprentice*.

Marketing is and marketers are often remote from the customers they are trying to reach, physically, psychologically and materially. Marketing information is used to try to close the gaps between us. The old Native American proverb 'to understand a person you must walk a day in their moccasins' applies here. We may feel that we are instinctively aware of our customers needs and desires the truth is that even without information companies still make decisions that fail to ask the most basic of questions. 'What is that we do that they, the customers, want?'

There are many examples of companies drifting away from their customers needs. Apple computers ion the early 1990s, Marks and Spencer in the early 2000s are high-profile examples of this.

Marketing information and research is used at each stage of the marketing planning process to ensure that better decisions are made about the marketing process

Mission

Vision and Values

Corporate Objectives

Situation Analysis

Internal Analysis – SWOT ———→ ←——— External Analysis – PESTEL

Key Issues

Objectives

Strategy Evaluation

Segmentation Targeting Positioning

Marketing Mix

Resource Allocation

Measurement

Controls and Evaluations

Figure 1.1: The marketing planning process

First of all, research and the database can also work at the corporate level. Research will help determine the nature and scope of the organization, and may be used in developing the mission and values of an organization. Research and the database will be used significantly in the PEST and SWOT analysis. They will help us to:

◆ Understand the current attitudes and opinions of our customers

◆ Define our distinctive competence relative to competitive companies

◆ Determine future strategies for the business by looking at markets and customers, segmentation and our brands, products and services

◆ Measure and evaluate the effectiveness of our activity.

Research and the database inform the configuration of the marketing mix . Chisnall talks about this in his book (Chisnall, 2004). He shows that research works at each of four areas of the marketers' responsibilities. These are:

1 **Analysis** – Identify market trends, competitors' activities, customer preferences in existing and potential markets.

2 **Planning** – Decide on a range of products and services likely to satisfy identified needs present and emergent.

3 **Control** – Check that standards of performance are maintained.

4 **Implementation** – Organize development, production and distribution of specific products and services.

Of course, the database also works at all these levels.

This list is useful but not exhaustive. A more comprehensive list is provided in Crouch and Housden's book on market research and this is outlined below (Crouch and Housden, 2003):

Corporate planning

Information is used in corporate planning in order to make decisions about what goals the organization, as a whole, should have in both the short and long term:

◆ Forecasting the size of future demand and trends for the organization's products

◆ Identifying markets to be served

◆ Assessing the strengths and weaknesses of the organization both absolutely and relative to its competitors

◆ Measuring dissatisfaction and needs in relevant market segments

◆ Industry/market structure and composition

◆ Competitor, market share and profitability analysis

◆ Highlighting significant marketing problems

◆ Stimulating research for new or exploitation of existing products and markets by planned policies

◆ Evaluating corporate identity and image

◆ Selecting companies for acquisition or divestment.

Customer research:

◆ Identifying, measuring and describing key market segments' behaviour and attitudes

◆ Assessing relative profitability of markets over time

◆ Analysis and interpretation of general market data

◆ Placing individual customer transactions, perhaps recorded on a database, in the broader market context

◆ Analysing business potential of new market areas

◆ Identifying and evaluating markets for products and new products for markets

◆ Measuring consumer preferences

◆ Identifying changes in competitive activity

◆ Sales forecasting.

Product planning (including packaging and service levels)

Research and the database may be used in making and adapting products to fulfil customer wants more accurately and profitably:

◆ Generating and screening new product ideas and modifications

◆ Concept testing

◆ Product testing and re-testing for acceptance and improvement

◆ Testing formulation and presentation preferences

◆ Packaging tests

◆ Product name tests

◆ Test marketing

◆ Comparative testing against competitive products

◆ Product elimination or product line simplification

◆ Evaluating perceived service quality.

Promotional planning

Research and the database may be concerned with the selection and effectiveness of persuasive communications. Two main areas are identified below:

Communications planning

◆ Developing sustainable brand positioning

◆ Message design and content

◆ Development of the creative proposition

◆ Developing effective multimedia communications strategies online and offline

◆ Pre-testing ads

◆ Post-testing ads, for example awareness, comprehension, recall, attitude shifts, brand-switching effects

- Advertising weight-of-expenditure tests
- Media planning: evaluation, selection and scheduling
- Advertising effectiveness
- Public relations and publicity effects on awareness/attitude
- Sponsorship effectiveness
- Exhibition effectiveness research
- Direct marketing effectiveness research
- Assessing the impact of integration
- Developing the optimum communications mix.

Sales force planning

- Determining sales areas
- Testing alternative selling techniques and messages
- Setting sales targets
- Evaluating sales performance
- Evaluating sales compensation system
- Making selling operations more productive.

Distribution planning

Research and the database may be concerned with the formulation and effectiveness of distribution policy:

- Channel selection
- Distribution cost analysis
- Wholesaler/retailer margin
- Incentive policy
- Dealer sales levels
- Distribution achievement
- Penetration levels
- Stock checks
- Inventory policy.

Price planning

Research and the database may help as one of the inputs to price selection.

So what is marketing research?

Alan Wilson (2006) in the course text defines marketing research as:

The collection, analysis and communication of information undertaken to assist decision-making in marketing.

This picks up on the essential characteristics of marketing research, that is, the gathering and analysis of information to inform decisions. This decision-making aspect is important. Marketing research should enable decision-making.

Some authors would argue that a decision MUST result from the marketing research process, and in practice this is most often the case, even if the decision is to do nothing!

Wilson (2006) identifies four key characteristics of marketing research. These are are:

1   Generates information to aid marketing decision-making

2   Involves the collection of information

3   Involves the analysis of information

4   Involves the communications and dissemination of information.

We will look at each of these areas in detail as we work through the text.

Definitions

There are a number of other definitions and we need to look at these.

Perhaps the most important from the UK perspective is that of the Market Research Society (MRS). The MRS is the professional body overseeing professional standards in the marketing research industry in the United Kingdom (more about them later).

Marketing research is defined by the MRS (2008) as:

The collection and analysis of data from a sample of individuals or organizations relating to their characteristics, behaviour, attitudes, opinions or possessions. It includes all forms of marketing and social research such as consumer and industrial surveys, psychological investigations, observational and panel studies.

As you can see and as you might expect, it is much more technical. It covers techniques and sector applications. Do not worry now if you do not understand terms like 'sample', or 'observational and panel studies'. You will by the time you finish the coursebook!

Less formally, the MRS (2008) says that:

Research is one of the most useful tools in business, any business. It is the way in which organizations find out what their customers and potential customers need, want and care about. This involves the collection and interpretation of confidential data concerning people, products, services and organizations. The key elements in obtaining good research material are that researchers talk to a few people to get the views of many, and that it only works if they talk to the right number of people, ask the right questions and interpret the results correctly.

Research has a variety of uses, from the testing of new products, to employment and customer satisfaction surveys, to social and opinion research. It can help organizations and individuals identify new market areas and assess the scope and

potential success of a particular advertising/marketing campaign and develop new policies and future activities.

One of the biggest growth areas for research over the past few years has been in the field of opinion research – understanding more about the public's view on social topics such as politics, the environment, religion, and moral issues.

The American Marketing Association's early definition sounds like Alan Wilson's. In the past, the American Marketing Association (1961) defined research as:

The systematic gathering, recording and analysing of data relating to problems in the marketing of goods and services.

They changed this definition. Why do you think they did? The word 'problems' causes some difficulties. Marketing research is also about identifying opportunities for growth in business. They changed it to the following – notice they included 'opportunities' this time.

Marketing research is the function that links the consumer, customer and public to the marketer through information – information used to identify and define marketing opportunities and problems; generate, refine and evaluate marketing actions; monitor marketing performance; and improve understanding of marketing as a process. Marketing research specifies the information required to address these issues, designs the method for collecting information, manages and implements the data collection process, analyses the results, and communicates the findings and their implications. (American Marketing Association, 2005)

How about the CIM? They too have their own definitions. This is taken from the website www.cim.co.uk, which has a useful glossary of marketing terms. You should add this to your browser's favourites list.

The CIM (2008) defines marketing research as:

The gathering and analysis of data relating to market places or customers; any research which leads to more market knowledge and better-informed decision-making.

You may have noticed by now that the definitions refer to marketing and market research almost interchangeably. The distinction is not important. Market research has come to be seen as a subset of marketing research. Market research refers to research on markets whereas marketing research covers the broad scope of marketing activity.

The database and marketing research

Marketing research does not exist in isolation. There is a great deal of pertinent information held on company databases. Alan Wilson (2006) defines the marketing database as:

A manual or computerized source of data relevant to marketing decision-making about an organization's customers.

There are a few things about this definition that need to be explained.The database does not have to be computer-based. It can be kept on hard copy. However, access to database technology is very easy and cheap. Even the cheapest and simplest software is capable of storing a significant number of records. Microsoft Access is perfectly serviceable for many businesses.

While the definition limits itself to 'customers' other definitions spell out the fact that the database will collect data about past and potential customers as well as current customers. De Tienne and Thompson (1996) use the following definition of database marketing:

The process of systematically collecting in electronic or optical form data about past, current and/or potential customers, maintaining the integrity of the data by continually monitoring customer purchases and/or by inquiring about changing status and using the data to formulate marketing strategy and foster personalized relationships with customers.

The IDM defines the marketing database as:

A comprehensive collection of inter-related customer and/or prospect data that allows the timely accurate retrieval, use or manipulation of that data to support the marketing objectives of the enterprise. (Downer, 2002)

Wilson (2006) suggests that marketers develop customer databases for four reasons:

1   To personalize marketing communications

2   To improve customer service

3   To understand customer behaviour

4   To assess the effectiveness of the organization's marketing and service activities.

What should be clear is that marketing research and the database should work together to provide information to decisions makers.

The role of information

Wilson (2006) outlines the nature of marketing information. Information may be useful at a variety of levels within the organization and may be applied in a variety of ways to aid strategic, operational and tactical decisions.

Information may be:

◆   Descriptive

   ◆ What

   ◆ Where

   ◆ When

◆   Comparative

   ◆ How does this differ

   ◆ How does it compare

◆   Diagnostic

   ◆ Why do they do this

   ◆ Why do they believe

◆   Predictive

   ◆ What would happen if

The growth in information sources

At the heart of all successful enterprises is managed information. This may come from marketing research or from the customer database but, as Alan Wilson points out in the module's core text, it is integration that is important.

Integrated information is critical to effective decision-making. Marketing information sources can be thought of as separate jigsaw pieces; only when they are connected does the whole picture become clear. Taking decisions by looking at each of the pieces individually is not only inefficient but is likely to result in wrong assumptions and decisions being made (Wilson, 2006).

The role of knowledge management

The role of knowledge management within organizations has become central to the delivery of the above definition of marketing orientation. Tom Peters and Robert Waterman (1995) in their influential book *In Search Of Excellence* attempted to identify the characteristics of successful companies. Published in 1995, at the beginning of the information revolution, the book identified customer focus and knowledge acquired largely through the use of marketing research as central to the success of the companies they researched.

Since 1995 many of the companies they researched have gone out of business or no longer exist in the same structure!

However, the point that they made is still valid. In the *FT* on 18 November 2003, Charlie Dawson wrote:

> *The way to make a difference is to get managers to see the world from the customers' perspective ... with the right set up guided by formal research it can change their world ... (however) the customer never makes it beyond the research chart or the mission statement. Given this context market research is bound to fail. It is the market researchers who connect with customers but then have to turn their learning into meeting fodder.*

What we see here is that advantage in the marketplace does not simply come from carrying out research, it is about identifying, collating, understanding, analysing and acting upon the many diverse sources of knowledge within an organization. Many organizations, however, are still not geared up to manage this process effectively. What is required is a significant cultural and internal organizational change. However, many companies find this change very difficult to manage.

Baker and Mouncey (2003) describe this as a problem faced by many businesses locked, as they say, in a 'cultural prison'.

> *We have been struck by how repetitive some of the messages have been and found ourselves asking why so little change has followed. We would offer the view that the industry has not moved quickly enough and appears to have been struck by a level of inertia characteristic of 'cultural prisoners' – those who find themselves doing things the way they've always been done simply because that's the way they've always been done. Are there any 'cultural architects' within the industry in a position to move now to build a brighter future?*

What these organizations find is that they are unable to gear up the knowledge capital that has been established within their business.

Data silos

Customer information may exist in silos that are not connected, leading to vital gaps in understanding and failure to provide basic service standards. As we will see later, when customers give us information they expect us to use it responsibly and to improve levels of service to them. These organizations may find that knowledge rests with individuals or departments within the company and that these assets are fiercely protected. For example, sales people or key account managers may see the introduction of a marketing database as a serious threat to their position rather than a means by which their efficiency and effectiveness (and their commissions) may be improved.

These multiple systems, for example, separate sales, accounts and fulfilment databases operating under different protocols and on different platforms cost money to run and maintain and lead to duplication and wastefulness, disillusioned staff and very often, the research tells us, unhappy and poorly served customers. Equally the lack of systems for capturing and storing information means that when key personnel leave an organization they take their knowledge with them.

The aim of knowledge management

The aim of knowledge management is to integrate systems and individuals to enable and encourage knowledge transfer between employees and other stakeholders. For example, knowledge management systems may work between retailers and their suppliers to ensure 'just-in-time' delivery of new stock, to plan and implement sales promotion campaigns and to jointly manage the marketing research that underpins new product development.

In the UK, Tesco is an excellent example of a company that gears up its knowledge assets to produce value for itself, its stakeholders and its customers. Knowledge is often defined as distinct from information. Whilst much of this is semantics the key distinguishing factor is that knowledge is not data. Data are facts; knowledge involves interpreting, analysing and understanding facts to produce actionable intelligence.

The aim of knowledge management is to:

◆   Identify where knowledge resides within an organization

◆   Develop mechanisms for capturing, documenting, enhancing or augmenting this knowledge

◆   Transferring and sharing this knowledge and

◆   Finally using the knowledge to improve marketing and business performance.

Activity 1.5

You are the research and insight manager for a large food manufacturer. Outline the sources of knowledge that might feed a knowledge management system.

In the next chapter we will look in detail at the role of the database and decision-support systems in managing the knowledge assets of companies. The decision-support system contains the tools needed to make sense of data; it may include statistical packages and an intranet with a range of tools and information to help marketers make decisions.

The issue that many companies face is simply too much information. Tesco, through their data analysis company Dunn Humby, manages this very well. They transform huge amounts of data into very simple clearly understood strategic imperatives. The information revolution has meant an increasingly degree of complexity for marketing managers and the idea of transforming data into actionable intelligence should lie at the heart of information strategy

The Internet, intranets and extranets

The Internet has changed the nature of the research and information business. Increasingly it is possible to access reliable information from a variety of providers online and to distribute this information via intranets within the organization and extranets with preferred partners outside.

Online communities, discussion boards and blogs

The Internet has created a new revolution in information. The number of blogs and discussion forums is put conservatively at around 100 million and some of these will relate to brands, products and services.

Activity 1.6

Go to www.technorati.com and www.boardtracker.com and review the blogs for your product or area of interest.

Social networking

Social networking sites such as Face Book and other social networking sites are increasingly being used by businesses to help them understand and talk to customers.

Facebook has been reported as making user profiles available to business and the commercial spin offs of these sites have yet to be fully realized.

Activity 1.7

Look at the following sites. What commercial applications can you imagine for your business?

Face book	www.facebook.com
You tube	www.youtube.com
My space	www.myspace.com
Flickr	www.flickr.com
Twitter	www.twitter.com
Bebo	www.bebo.com

Summary

This unit has introduced the concepts of marketing and the information that enables effective management of the marketing function in all organizations.

The definition of marketing as the management process responsible for identifying, anticipating and satisfying customer needs profitably means that timely, accurate and pertinent information underpins marketing orientation.

We explored the role of marketing research and the database as the keys to delivering effective marketing plans.

We looked at a number of different definitions of marketing research and database marketing. Marketing research was defined as 'the collection and analysis of data from a sample of individuals or organizations relating to their characteristics, behaviour, attitudes, opinions or possessions. It includes all forms of marketing and social research such as consumer and industrial surveys, psychological investigations, observational and panel studies' (MRS, 2007).

We looked at this definition in detail and outlined the scope of marketing research within the organization, centring on the planning process.

We finally looked at the growth of the knowledge economy and the role of the Internet, Intra and extra nets in marketing information and research.

We also considered online communities and social networking sites.

Bibliography

American Marketing Association (1961) *Report of the Definitions Committee*, Chicago: AMA (quoted in Chisnall, 2004)

Baker, S. and Mouncey, P. (2003) The market researcher's manifesto, *International Journal of Market Research*, 45 (4)

Chisnall, P. (2004) *Marketing Research*, McGraw-Hill, 7th edition

Crouch, S. and Housden, M. (2003) *Marketing Research for Managers*, Oxford: Elsevier Butterworth-Heinemann, 3rd edition

Davenport, T. and Prusak, L. (1998) *Working Knowledge: How Organizations Manage What They Know*, Harvard Business School Press (quoted in Yahya and Goh, 2002)

Davidson, H. (1997) *Even More Offensive Marketing*, Harmondsworth: Penguin

Dawson, C. (2003) Creative business, *Financial Times*, 18 November

De Tienne, K. and Thompson, J. (1996) Database marketing and organizational learning theory: towards and research agenda, *Journal of Consumer Marketing*, 13 (5)

Downer, G. (2002) The interactive and Direct Marketing Guide, www.micromarketing-online.com The IDM.

Johnson, G., Scholes, K. and Whittington, R. (2008) *Exploring Corporate Strategy: Text and cases*, FT Prentice Hall, 8th edition

Jones, T. and Sasser, W. (1995) Why satisfied customers defect, *Harvard Business Review*, November-December, pp. 88-99

Kanter, R. M. (1984) *The Change Masters*, London: Allen and Unwin

Malhotra, Y. (1998) Deciphering the knowledge management hype, *Journal for Quality and Participation*, 21 (quoted in Yahya and Goh, 2002)

MRS (2007) Code of Conduct

Peters, T. and Waterman, R. (1995) *In Search of Excellence*, Profile Business

Reichheld, F. (2001) *The Loyalty Effect: The Hidden Force Behind Growth Profits and Lasting Value*, Harvard Business School Press

Wilson, A. (2006) *Marketing Research, An Integrated Approach*, FT Prentice Hall, 2nd edition

Yahya, S. and Goh, W. (2002) Managing human resources for knowledge management, *Journal of Knowledge Management*, 6 (5)

Websites

American Marketing Association (2005) www.marketingpower.com

CIM (2008) www.cim.co.uk

MRS (2007) www.mrs.org.uk/standards/codeconduct.htm

Lloyds (2008) www.lloyds.com

www.dma.org

www.esomar.org

Unit 2
The database and CRM

Learning objectives

By the end of this unit you will be able to:

◆ Evaluate the impact of information technology on the marketing function and discuss the challenges facing organizations in collecting valid, reliable and measurable information to support the decision-making process.

◆ Explain the concept of a marketing decision support system and its role in supporting marketing decisions.

◆ Demonstrate an understanding of the role, application and benefits of customer databases in relation to customer relationship management (CRM).

◆ Identify and explain the different stages in the process of setting up a database.

◆ Explain the principles of data warehousing, data marts and data mining.

◆ Explain the relationship between database marketing and marketing research and explain the legal aspects of data collection and usage, including the data protection legislation.

Table 2.1: Learning outcomes and knowledge and skills requirements

Learning outcomes	Knowledge and skills requirements
1.2 Evaluate the impact of information technology on the marketing function and discuss the challenges facing organizations in collecting valid, reliable and measurable information to support the decision-making process	Customer databases Internal reporting system, scanning/inventory control, etc. Validity and reliability of different information sources
1.3 Explain the concept of a marketing decision support system and its role in supporting marketing decisions	Definition Components (data storage, reports and displays, analysis and modelling) Types of information held Manner in which it can assist decision making
2.1 Demonstrate an understanding of the role, application and benefits of customer databases in relation to customer relationship management (CRM)	Types of customer data (behavioural data, volunteered data, attributed data) Role in profiling customers Role in marketing intelligence testing campaigns/ forecasting Role in determining life-time value Role in personalizing offerings and communications Role in building relationships
2.2 Identify and explain the different stages in the process of setting up a database	The importance of evaluating software and what is needed to ensure it works properly Evaluating software Identifying needs of users of a database Processing data (formatting, validation, de-duplication)
2.3 Explain the principles of data warehousing, data marts and data mining	Understanding how databases can be used to select, explore and model large amounts of data to identify relationships and patterns of behaviour
2.4 Explain the relationship between database marketing and marketing research and explain the legal aspects of data collection and usage, including the data protection legislation	Data protection legislation List brokers Profilers and their offerings (eg, Acorn, Mosaic, etc.) Issues involved in merging marketing research and customer database information (transparency, aggregation of data, using customer databases for marketing research purposes)

Key definitions

The marketing database – A manual or computerized source of data relevant to marketing decision-making about an organization's customers (Wilson, 2006).

Behavioural data – Data that is derived directly from the behaviour of the customer.

Volunteered data – Data that is given up by the customer through, for example, registering on a website.

Profile data – Data that is obtained by linking the database with other sources of information.

Attributed data – Data that is extrapolated from the results of market research.

Golden fields – The key information elements of the database that must be completed and maintained for good database marketing.

Lifestyle data – Lifestyle companies collect information on customers' lifestyles. The data is assembled from various sources; guarantee cards filled in, in return for an extended warranty; questionnaires inserted in magazines or mailed to previous respondents; competition entry forms and so on (Thomas and Housden, 2003).

Geo-demographics – Companies supply a system of categorizing the country into a number of different demographic types. Each postcode in the country is assigned one of these types. This means that each customer on your database can be matched to a demographic type. When this is done across all of your customer records, a demographic profile emerges (Thomas and Housden, 2003).

Data capture – Information taken on to a computer system.

Deduplication – System of removing names and addresses which appear in a list more than once.

OLAP – Online analytical processing.

Customer relationship management (CRM) – An integrated approach to identifying, acquiring and retaining customers. By enabling organizations to manage and coordinate customer interactions across multiple channels, departments, lines of business and geographies, CRM helps organizations maximize the value of every customer interaction and drive superior corporate performance (Siebel, 2003).

Study guide

This unit should take you around three hours. You should add another three hours for supplementary reading and case studies.

The marketing database

We defined the marketing database in Unit 1. Can you remember any of the definitions?

The course textbook by Alan Wilson (2006) defines the database as: 'A manual or computerized source of data relevant to marketing decision-making about an organization's customers'.

De Tienne and Thompson (1996) use this definition of database marketing:

The process of systematically collecting in electronic or optical form data about past, current and/or potential customers, maintaining the integrity of the data by continually monitoring customer purchases and/or by inquiring about changing status and using the data to formulate marketing strategy and foster personalized relationships with customers.

The IDM defines the marketing database as:

A comprehensive collection of inter-related customer and/or prospect data that allows the timely, accurate, retrieval, use or manipulation of that data to support the marketing objectives of the enterprise. (Downer, 2002)

Activity 2.1

We have three definitions. What are the common characteristics that link them?

What data is held on a database?

Alan Wilson (2006) identifies four types of customer data:

◆ **Behavioural data** – This is derived directly from the behaviour of the customer.

◆ **Volunteered data** – Data that is given up by the customer through – for example, registering on a website.

◆ **Profile data** – This data is obtained by linking our database with other sources of information. They are linked by commonly held data – for example, name, address or postcode. For example, Mosaic (see below).

◆ **Attributed data** – This is data that is extrapolated from the results of market research. Although held anonymously, the results of research on a small sample of the database can be flagged against the entire database. For example, a survey that looked at attitudes by age group could be used to group all customers into a relevant segment.

What does this mean in practice? We have all heard of information overload. So in that case what data should a database contain? Clearly there will be a difference between B2C and B2B markets.

Activity 2.2

The list below presents six categories of data that might be collected. Try to flesh out the list. Under each heading write as many types of information that you may need to inform marketing decisions. What are the implications for B2B markets?

Identification data   Demographic data

Financial data   Lifestyle data

Transactional data   Other data

If the differences are immediate then there are many similarities. There are standard elements and these are generally the 'golden' fields, which should be completed and maintained for good database marketing. Clearly these include identification data and the fields that cover customers' behaviour. Generally the most important categories here are recency, frequency, amount and product category, as this data helps us to model the value of the database now and into the future through the use of lifetime value analysis.

The key fields for any database will be different from the next due to the different business contexts and objectives the data supports. There is clearly a need to collect data that is reliable and accurate and that supports current and future decision making.

The temptation is to capture and hold as much data as possible about customers but remember that every piece of information needs to be maintained and there is a cost in acquiring and maintaining data. As we will see later there is a legal obligation on companies to ensure that data is sufficient and not excessive and also is kept up to date.

Some data will decay relatively quickly, for example, buying patterns and consumption data may change minute by minute, other data will change slowly, for example job title or address. Other data should change rarely or not at all, for example, gender and date of birth. Although sometime even this does change! Attitudinal data will also change slowly. For example, consider your attitudes to the death penalty. They were probably formed when you became aware of these issues in your early teens and have probably not changed. Similar data can be powerful in terms of creating brand propositions.

Where does data come from?

Data is obtained from a range of sources. Some of these are planned and managed and some are as a result of the day-to-day operation of the business. Data that comes as a result of the day-to-day activity of the business may include:

◆ Accounts records

◆ Sales force reports

◆ Service records

◆ Reports from intermediaries

◆ Customer enquiries or complaints

◆ Responses to marketing communications

◆ Guarantee cards.

Any contact with a customer of prospect is an opportunity of data capture. The data strategy must be established in order to ensure that these opportunities are appraised effectively and that relevant data is captured consistently and constantly.

Information that is generated from planned activity includes:

◆ Bought lists

◆ Industry sector reports

◆ Primary marketing research

◆ Competitor analyses

◆ Responses to exhibitions and public relations events.

What do we do with data?

Customer profiling

Working with our data can help a great deal in terms of creating a more efficient and more effective marketing strategy. Profiling of customers can tell us:

◆   Who are the most profitable customers and their characteristics

◆   How to create smaller profitable segments

◆   Which are most likely to respond

◆   Who has greatest potential.

This means we can create:

◆   More relevant sales messages

◆   Smaller volume of activity with less wastage

◆   Better response levels and ROI.

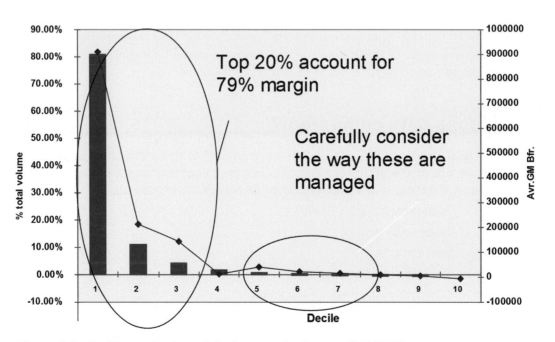

Figure 2.1: Profiling: value-based decile analysis. *Source*: IDM 2008.

Source: © The IDM Diploma in Interactive and Direct Marketing. www.theidm.com

We can carry out a range of techniques to help us model and understand data more effectively. Some of these lie outside the course but the use of data modelling can help reveal insight from data and help the effectiveness of strategies.

Techniques include:

◆   Simple regression analysis

◆   Cluster analysis

◆   CHAID – chi-squared automatic interaction detection

◆   Neural networks – a complex 'black box' system, beyond the scope of this course.

Regression analysis

Regression analysis scores individuals according to their characteristics. For example, buyers of a certain product may have certain other characteristics. They may:

◆   Live in certain areas

◆   Have certain income levels

◆   Have a certain number of children.

By applying this to all records and scoring those records, we can predict those with the highest scores have a greater tendency to buy. We will look at regression later in the coursebook.

Cluster analysis

This groups customers according to their general characteristics. This can be used to create segments from the database.

CHAID

This is used to break down the customer base into segments based on certain key variables. It is used to target subgroups on the database more effectively. Thomas and Housden (2003) give a good example of how this works.

Case study: Using the CHAID model

To understand the workings of CHAID, let us consider a bank wishing to sell ISAs. At present, 8 per cent of customers have an ISA and they wish to increase this to 10 per cent. The CHAID model is fed, say 30,000 customer records containing data on:

◆   Number of ISAs

◆   Household income

◆   Size of mortgage

◆   Years as a customer and so on.

The CHAID software considers all of the given variables and determines which is the most important in this case.

Let us say it establishes that the most significant factor is 'years as a customer'. It further subdivides this factor into, say: less than 1 year with the bank; 1 to 5 years as a customer; more than 5 years. It may then identify something like the following:

◆   Less than 1 year as a customer – only 3 per cent have an ISA

◆   1 to 5 years – 8 per cent have an ISA

◆   More than 5 years – 12 per cent have an ISA.

The CHAID model then moves on to the next stage which is to take each of these three segments and considers the next most significant variable in each instance.

It may ascertain that in the most loyal customer segment (more than 5 years with the bank) the next best discriminator is mortgage size. People in this segment with mortgages of more than £100,000 may have a 14 per cent take-up of ISAs.

By breaking down each segment into its significant variables, a number of potentially good sub-segments may emerge.

The output is a tree diagram (Figure 2.2) and we can select/deselect by the segments:

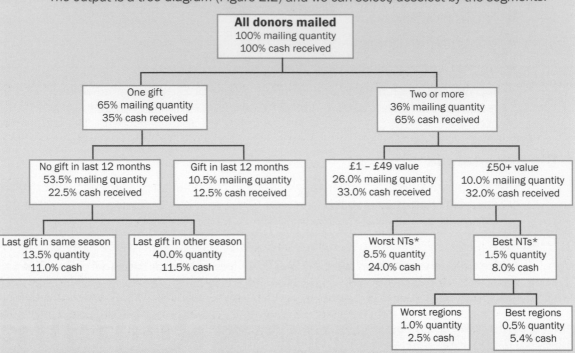

Figure 2.2: A CHAID analysis of charity donors. *Source*: ©The IDM 2008. www.theidm.com

* NTs represent a geo-demographic neighbourhood type.

The analysis shows that the number of previous gifts would have been the best variable: 36 per cent who sent 2 or more donations account for 65 per cent of the money.

This model shows 88.5 per cent of the cash could have been raised from just 60 per cent of the mailing list.

10.5% yields	12.5% cash
26.0% yields	33% cash
10.0% yields	32% cash
13.5% yields	11% cash
60% volume =	88.5% cash

Geo-demographic and lifestyle profiling

Geo-demographic and lifestyle profiling is a useful addition to the marketers' armoury. Once we have data, it can be enhanced through overlaying bought-in data. This can be bought from, for example, Experian who runs the Mosaic system, CACI who run ACORN and Acxiom who run a number of different data products including the Personicx profiling system. Eurodirect owns the Cameo suite of products. Dunn and Bradstreet, Information Arts and Blue Sheep offer profiling and other services in the B2B market.

Activity 2.3

Visit the following websites and teview the services that these companies offer:

www.experian.com   www.acxiom.co.uk

www.caci.co.uk   www.dnb.com.

www.eurodirect.co.uk   www.information-arts.com

www.bluesheep.com

The way the services work is to run your data against the service specified and a code is appended to your records. This can link with a range of other data; for example, Mosaic codes will link to a variety of other data sources including TGI which we will discuss later.

Lifestyle classification works normally on researched lists. Acxiom, for example, collects data from the domestic appliances warranty registration cards filled in by new customers.

Geo-demographics works on the idea that 'birds of a feather flock together' and that customers who share postcodes will share behavioural characteristics.

You can see this with the Mosaic classifications at group level below. Mosaic divides households in the country into 11 groups and 61 types. The classification is based in large part on census data but also includes other data sources. According to MOSAIC, 54 per cent of the data used to build Mosaic is sourced from the 2001 Census. The remaining 46 per cent is derived from their consumer segmentation database, which provides coverage of all of the UK's 46 million adult residents and 23 million households. It includes:

◆   The edited Electoral Roll

◆   Experian Lifestyle Survey information, and Consumer Credit Activity

◆   The Post Office Address File

◆   Shareholders Register

◆   House Price and Council Tax information

◆   ONS local area statistics

Source: www.business-strategies.co.uk/

The Mosaic system's 11 groups are:

◆   Symbols of Success

◆   Happy Families

◆   Suburban Comfort

◆   Ties of Community

◆   Urban Intelligence

◆   Welfare Borderline

◆   Municipal Dependency

◆   Blue Collar Enterprise

◆   Twilight Subsistence

◆   Grey Perspectives

◆   Rural Isolation

Mosaic offers a significant range of services including Commercial Mosaic for B2B profiling and consumer products covering Scotland, Northern Ireland and London, as well as sector activities covering financial services, grocery, automotive and public sector markets.

The census happens every 10 years in the UK. In the past, census data was gathered from what are called Enumeration Districts of about 150 households and then translated into postcode areas. The 2001 data is presented in what are called output areas and is postcode based. It is this data that the Mosaic system now uses. Other geo-demographic systems, for example, ACORN work in a similar way.

Variations of the ACORN system have been introduced to serve the classification needs of specific markets. These include:

◆ Health ACORNLifestyles UK

◆ Scottish ACORN

◆ Northern Irish ACORN

◆ Financial ACORN.

A cut-down example of one of the Mosaic classifications can be seen below. Whilst there are some weaknesses in the approach, you can see that in certain markets the use of this data would be very helpful.

Insight: Group A – Symbols of success

Type A06: High Technologists

Summary

High Technologists are found in areas of modern, high specification family housing, mostly in outer metropolitan areas, which attract well-paid executives working in large corporations.

Demography

This type contains many areas of new wealth where larger corporations, many of which are based in the high technology sector, recruit highly paid executives to manufacture products or services with a high value added content.

Environment

Neighbourhoods of High Technologists tend to consist of quite large detached houses, mostly of modern design, laid out in quiet cul-de-sacs and in relatively small developments. Houses are typically arranged in an irregular manner and many of the designs, though they use common components, look as though they are one-off. These tend mostly to be open plan estates and many residents have difficulty fitting their cars into the private space available.

Economy

Neighbourhoods of High Technologists are scattered throughout the country but occur in largest numbers in the triangle between Newbury, Basingstoke and Windsor within the commuter hinterland of Oracle and Microsoft. Whilst by no means all the residents work in high-tech industries, these are very much areas where corporate executives work in a high-tech office environment and need to be confident in coping with automation.

Consumer values

High Technologists typically approach consumer decisions from a rational perspective and value brands that offer high levels of flexibility and personalization and convey an image of innovation and high performance.

Consumption patterns

High Technologists have high levels of disposable incomes, not least as a result of the benefits such as company cars and pension and insurance schemes to which many of them are entitled. These are good markets for home furnishings, for new kitchens, bathrooms, conservatories and extensions and for electronic equipment particularly relating to home entertainment and information technology.

Change

The age profile of High Technologists areas will continue to age, though once residents get to retirement age it is likely that many of them will move to more rural locations.

Source: Experian, 2007

Mosaic also works at a European level and has a number of other targeting tools that the marketer can use.

Thomas and Housden (2003) suggest a general rule as to the hierarchy of data held on the database:

1   **Your own customer data** – most powerful as it relates to your customers and their existing relationship with you.

2   **Lifestyle data** – as it relates to individuals by name and address.

3   **Demographic data** – dealing as it does with the characteristics of neighbourhoods rather than households.

The process of setting up a marketing database

The process of setting up a database is complex and demanding. A staged planning approach is outlined below.

1   Business review

2   Data audit

3   Data strategy and specification

4   Data verification

5   Hardware/software

6   Data capture, maintenance and enhancement

7   Management issues – should the database be run in-house/out-of-house?

8   Applications

9   Review.

Business review

It is important that the overall mission and objectives are reviewed in order to inform the process of establishing the database. It could be that a database is not required to fulfil the mission of the business or that the cost of a particular database design or hardware is too great. All business decisions should begin with an understanding of the strategic direction of the business. The database decision is no exception. We must ask:

◆ How will data help the business achieve its business and marketing objectives?

◆ Where will the business be in 10 years' time?

◆ What media, information and technology changes need to be built into the system?

◆ What segments will the data support now and in the future?

◆ What business processes will the database support?

◆ How will the database be accessed?

◆ Is the database open to customers through the Internet?

The data audit

Carrying out an in-depth data audit is the next stage of the process. We need to establish the following:

◆ What information requirements does the organization have now and in the future?

◆ Where is this information held currently?

◆ What unnecessary information is currently held?

◆ How is this information currently used?

◆ How will it be used in future?

◆ Which departments and individuals need access to this information?

◆ If information is not available, where does it come from?

◆ Who will enter the data and ensure that is accurate and complete?

◆ What applications will this information support?

◆ How does the proposed system integrate with existing information management systems?

Data strategy, specification and verification

The review of strategy and the data audit should result in a long-term strategy for data within the organization. This should be capable of evolution and development over time as the markets served by the organization and the organization itself changes.

The strategy should specify the information that is required by the organization outlining where it is available and what additional data is to be acquired and managed.

It should determine the following:

◆ Who and what departments are able to use and update data held on the database?

◆ How will the data be kept up to date and who is responsible for this?

◆   What data verification rules will be put in place to ensure quality and completeness?

◆   What analysis systems will the database support?

Activity 2.4

Where will this data come from? Think about the ways that your company or a company of your choice may capture data on its customers. Write down as many data sources as you can.

Data needs to be kept up to date. This is a legal obligation under the 1998 Data Protection Act but is also vital for good practice in database marketing. Information has a life. It is estimated that professional marketers change their job every 18 months to three years. The lapse rates for trade press titles such as *Marketing* and *Marketing Week* are around 25–30 per cent. In the consumer market, data expires almost as quickly.

◆   People move house. About 10 per cent of households move house each year. The Royal Mail keeps a list of movers called the National Change of Address File (NCOA). The Postal Address File (PAF) will also help. This is a list of all 26.5 million addresses in the United Kingdom and is regularly updated.

◆   They die. It is dreadful to send mailings to dead people; it is ethically unacceptable and causes distress for families that have recently suffered bereavement. There are a number of services that help the marketer avoid this, for example The Bereavement Register and Mortascreen. For further details, go to the DMA website or the Royal Mail website.

◆   They are enticed away by the competition, by better, more relevant or cheaper offers.

◆   They leave due to poor marketing.

◆   They move out of the market; Club 18–30 has a clear target market!

◆   Their lifestyle changes, they marry or have children, or simply stop drinking or smoking or go on a diet.

◆   Their financial circumstances change, they trade up or trade down.

Case study: Telegraphing your renewal date

If you have taken out a subscription deal with the *Daily Telegraph*, you will have to decide at the end of your subscription period whether you wish to continue with the arrangement. The *Telegraph* knows from its database records when this decision will have to be made and they will mail you beforehand.

They will remind you what a great newspaper you read and restate the benefits of taking out a further subscription. The marketing database enables them to time these communications so that they are highly relevant to the individual recipients.

The *Telegraph* will not stop at simply sending you a simple reminder. They will also carry out anti-attrition studies. This is an important area – having gone to the considerable time and expense of recruiting a customer, one does not want to lose them through lack of understanding of their needs.

Many companies fail to carry on these simple procedures. Research from the Swedish Post Office shows that 65 per cent of customers leave because of a lack of contact from the company. This has been confirmed in another study by McGraw-Hill (Thomas and Housden, 2003).

Case study: Kimberly Clark

Kimberly Clark market the Huggies brand of nappies. Kimberly Clark has around two and a half years to sell the estimated 4500 nappies that the average child uses in this time. They try to ensure that every nappy used is a Huggies nappy. This involves a range of broad-scale communications and a series of data-driven targeted direct marketing communications. The Huggies Mother and Baby Club recruits members through the Bounty list, a list of expecting mothers that is compiled through responses to take ones and other media distributed to pregnant women. The women sign up for a range of free samples including Huggies nappies that are delivered after the delivery of the child. A series of targeted communications is also delivered to the family covering the period from the date of birth to potty training. Amongst these is a series of publications that provide information on care and other elements of child rearing. These include free samples and coupons. The publications are seen as valuable in themselves. They cover the following:

Step 1   Pregnancy

Step 2   Birth and early days

Step 3   Reaching out to the world

Step 4   Sitting up

Step 5   Crawling everywhere

Step 6   First steps

Step 7   Toddler days.

The publications deepen and strengthen the relationship between customers and the brand at a crucial time of life and the trust developed during this time sustains other brands in the Kimberly Clark family.

Data verification, capture, maintenance and enhancement

Data verification is important. A regular review of the data is important. Data fields should be reviewed to check that they are up to date and that they hold the data they are supposed to hold. We need to check if the data is usable and if not determine what we have to do to make use of the data? We also need to check that we do not hold duplicate data.

Deduplication

Deduplication is an important part of the process of verifying data. Duplication of records may occur for a number of reasons, including keystroke error or other data entry problems, or simply the fact that volunteered information is not provided in a consistent way.

We may have two addresses with slightly different names, for example:

Lewis K 128 Greene St SL6 8TY 12/8/62

Lewes Keith 128 Greene Ave SL6 8PY 12/8/62.

These may be different people or the same person. Deduplication ensures that we do not send multiple mailings or make repeat contacts in other ways. There are a number of software solutions that allow for deduplication of records. These packages can be set to different degrees of sensitivity and may be based on the number of matched characters and/or numbers or a string of digits or may allocate a weighting depending on the character of the data that is being assessed.

The two types of system are deterministic decision tables or probabilistic linking.

Deterministic decision tables evaluate data fields for degree of match and a letter grade is assigned, the grades form a match pattern which is looked up in a table to determine if a pair matches or not.

Lewis	K	128	Greene	St	SL6 8TY	12/8/62	
Lewes	Keith	128	Greene	Ave	SL6 8PY	12/8/62	
B	B	A	B	D	B	A	= BBABDBA
+5	+2	+3	+4	−1	+7	+9	= +29

In this example there is a high probability that these entries are for the same person.

Probabilistic linkages evaluate fields for degree of match and a weight is assigned that represents the informational content contributed by those values. The weights are summed to derive a total score that measures the reliability of the match.

The deduplication strategy will be determined by the cost of holding duplicate data and the cost of deduplicating this data and can be set for under or over kill.

Reference tables may be used to help the verification of data. Wilson (2006) gives examples of reference tables for titles, job description, brands, models of car and so on. These are crucial for the maintenance of data quality as they reduce errors.

Formatting will be used to ensure that data is entered consistently, that it fits the fields and is presented in consistent style. International databases have a range of issues around salutations, titles, address and postcode formats.

Verification and validation

It is important that data is entered correctly and is accurate; the process of verification and validation may mean that data is keyed in twice to ensure accuracy and where possible is verified against external data sources, for example, postal address data may be validated against the postal address file (PAF) run by the Royal Mail.

We may check that all product and communications codes are accurate by running entered data against a list of all codes. We may check to validate the range of data within a field, for example, income data may typically fall within a range of possible figures. Key stroke error may make the difference between thousands and millions!

Finally it is always recommended that a variety of data records are given a visual check.

Behind all data there will be an audit trail identifying when the data was captured, when it was last updated, etc.

Hardware and software

There are a range of vendors in the market. There are dozens of questions that need to be asked. The key questions are:

◆ Mainframe or PC

◆ Cost and time

◆ Integration with existing systems

◆ Scalability

◆ Do we have in-house expertise?

◆ Support offered

◆ Analysis systems support

◆ Maintenance costs

◆ Data capture, maintenance and enhancement

◆ Management issues – should the database be run in-house/out-of-house?

In-house or out-of-house

Database bureaux will host the database for your organization.

In-house operation has advantages and disadvantages:

Advantages

(a) Strategic orientation of the business should be assured.

(b) Integration and access is manageable.

(c) Greater control and ownership.

(d) Cost may be lower.

Disadvantages

(a) Cost of hardware and consultancy may be significant.

(b) Speed of development can be slow.

(c) Service standards may be lower than those from an out-of-house provider.

(d) Skills in IT and strategy may be weak.

(e) Specialist processing skills may not be readily available.

Database bureaux have the following advantages

(a) Skills and systems are developed and tested.

(b) No fixed costs: you pay for what you get.

(c) Speed: resources can be allocated to ensure prompt delivery and penalty clauses can be built in.

(d) Performance guarantees can be built into the contract.

Often there is migration from the bureau into the organization. This means that learning can take place at lower risk. The usual approach is outlined below:

(a) Set-up at the bureau

(b) Sort out data issues

(c) Set-up updates and enhancements

(d) Develop internally

(e) Run the two in parallel

(f) Import.

Applications

As we saw with the Tesco example, a huge amount of data may be captured by organizations. The key thing is to be able to analyse it.

How it all works – applications

Thomas and Housden (2003) put it simply in their book *Direct Marketing in Practice*:

Remember the marketing database is a series of tables. These can cover a huge range of data:

◆ A list of names and addresses

◆ A list of transactions

◆ A list of suppliers/delivery methods and so on

◆ A list of promotion codes

◆ A list of customers who have been mailed, and their responses or any logical collection of data.

For instance, it would not be logical to store details of every transaction against every customer in the same table. Some customers may have dozens of transactions, others only one. To avoid large areas of wasted space, transactions are stored in a separate table, with a link between the customer's name and address and the transaction.

Having assembled the data, records have to be selected for a particular mailing campaign. This is done by a process of raising queries. For instance, if we wished to mail customers who had spent more than £500 in the past six months we would:

◆ Tell the computer to identify all transactions of £500 or more between the dates XX and YY

◆ Link these transactions to the name and address table

◆ Get a count of how many names and addresses have been identified

◆ If required, extract the related names and addresses for use in the promotion.

Using queries in this way enables us to model campaigns and identify whether our selection parameters have been appropriate. If the count shows we have only 50 customers who fit the category (spent £500 within the last six months), we may wish to broaden the parameters.

We could extend the period to 12 months and/or reduce the qualifying total to £250. This would produce a larger number of prospects. The exact process used depends on the software being used. PC software is generally more user-friendly and allows the marketer to access the data directly. This makes modelling campaigns easier and quicker than was the case with mainframes and IT departments.

Using the data

The data can be used in a number of ways. The case below presents an outline of how the database works in financial services.

Insight: The database and financial services

The financial services sector is a heavy user of database analysis. Amongst others, a major bank has used their database in the following ways:

◆ To manage the branch network
- Identifying the most profitable branches
- Staff appraisal, monitoring, reward and recognition
- To identify staff training needs
- To manage branch location.

◆ To acquire new customers
- Through profiling of good, existing customers and using this
- To plan for the acquisition of new customers.
- To increase profitability of existing customers
- Reducing the cost of marketing
- Improved targeting
- Personalizing marketing communications
- Reduce attrition.

◆ Developing new products

◆ Developing new market segments.

◆ **Planning** – defining objectives, segmentation studies, targeting, campaign management analysis costs and return on investment.

◆ **Contacting customers** – which medium or combination of media is the most effective and efficient, at what time?

◆ **Data processing** – counts and reports to aid planning.

◆ **Production** – production of lists and labels for address management; producing lists for follow-up activities; merging letter copy and addresses.

◆ **Response handling** – recording responses to promotional mailings via unique tracking codes.

◆ **Lead processing** – tracking enquiries through 'to sale' and 'after sales'.

◆ **Campaign management** – customer paperwork and reports to help manage promotions.

◆ **Customer research** – information from questionnaires may be added to records to make the future planning process more effective.

◆ **Analysis** – pre-determined reports and other analysis.

Marketing applications of the database can be summed up as:

◆　Finding

◆　Acquiring

◆　Keeping

◆　Cross-selling additional products

◆　Up-selling higher value products

◆　Prevent inactivity

◆　Renewing

　　... customers!!

The marketing decision support system

Data warehouse and datamarts

There is a narrow but important difference between the database, data marts and data warehouses. In many ways they are different levels of the same thing – the range of data held on customers and marketing and other activity within an organization.

◆　A **data mart** is a collection of databases that may serve a particular purpose. These tend to be expensive to maintain as they duplicate information.

◆　**Data warehouses** are created to form a single view of the truth for the organization as a whole and consolidate data marts.

The creation of data warehousing may involve a complex reorganization of business processes. For example, one major manufacturing company had several different product codes for each component. The rationalization of these product codes was vital to enable sensible queries to be made of the data. The development of the data warehouse may be an expensive task especially around the integration of different systems and platforms. However, the advantages are clear and the enabling of complex decisions, not just at the marketing level, is one clear benefit. As the warehouse becomes more established, the level of decision-making it supports becomes higher. This allows the creation of a marketing decision support system.

We can see an example in Figure 2.3. Data is acquired from a variety of sources (silos). It is extracted, transformed and loaded (ETL), then analysed via OLAP systems (Online Analytical Processing), combined with other data sources and mined for insight. The results are used to drive further applications.

Typically an MDSS will facilitate the following:

◆　Customer interrogation

　　◆　Define contact rules and channel capacities

　　◆　Key events detection

　　◆　Analytics and propensity scoring

　　◆　Segmentation and selections

◆ Customer management

 ◆ Contact strategies

 ◆ Communications output

◆ Customer interactions

 ◆ Campaign and fulfilment management.

It is combined with a variety of tools to enable efficient and effective decisions to be made and often these are made automatically based on identified triggers. Below is a typical web- enabled display from Cameo, a data service from Eurodirect. It shows the creation of a selection for an online pet insurance product. There are a few prerequisites:

◆ A pet

◆ A computer

◆ A credit card

◆ High earnings as this is a discretionary purchase – 'CAMEO Investor' is a list of high net worth individuals

You can see that on this list the number of valid customers is just less than 1000 from an initial selection of over 3 million. A tremendous saving and far better targeted.

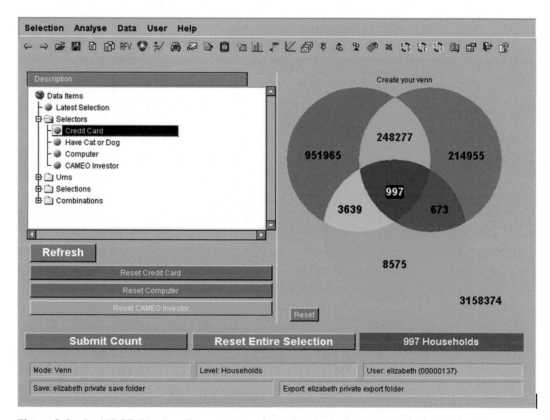

Figure2.3: An MDSS Display. Source: www.eurodirect.co.uk

Activity 2.5

Look at Cameo at www.eurodirect.co.uk

These support systems are far more sophisticated than the limited value from marketing information systems and companies like Alterian and Oracle are producing extremely sophisticated data-driven solutions to the active management of data. These can present, in a very accessible dashboard type display, a range of solutions to, for example, the creation of an e-mail campaign.

◆ Customer selections for e-mail campaigns

◆ The creation of copy and images to support the campaign

◆ Extranet access to control the creation of the campaign

◆ Access to click-through and open rates

◆ Final campaign metrics.

Activity 2.6

Look at www.alterian.com and explore the range of services they supply to the marketing industry.

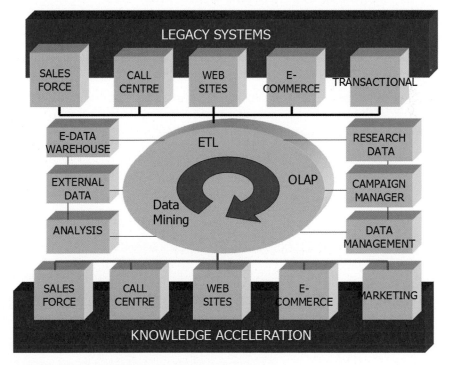

Figure2.4: Marketing decision support systems.

Source: IDM *Diploma in Interactive and direct marketing*

Activity 2.7

Visit the following websites and browse them to identify the range and nature of the claims for CRM and supporting systems. Bookmark them.

www.ibm.com

www.oracle.com/applications/crm/index.html

Data mining

Data mining is the process of analysing the database or the data warehouse to extract meaningful and actionable information. Antinou (1997) defines it as 'the process of extracting hidden and actionable information for large databases'. Data mining software can help this process. The process of analysis includes the process of statistical analysis of data or simple counts. It also includes a range of tools to help analyse the database. These are known as online analytical processing or OLAP.

Online analytical processing tools establish an analysis universe and allow for queries to be made of data, for example counts of the number of people of a certain age who bought a particular product. These tools allow us to drill into the database to analyse sub-samples in detail. This sample may be removed from the database and analysed offline.

Using the database for lifetime value analysis

Using the database allows us to answer some very important questions. Perhaps the most important of these is, what is the value of a customer over time? If we are capturing key financial data such as when a customer last bought from us, how much they spend and how regularly they spend, we can calculate this.

Customer lifetime value (CLTV) will vary according a number of factors including the way the customer was recruited, including media and offer, the type of product purchased and a range of other key factors. We use CLTV to help in a number of areas:

◆ To justify spend on new customers

◆ To evaluate the quality of media and offers

◆ To help with marketing segmentation

◆ To help measure the output of retention programmes.

For example, Tesco used CLTV analysis to help justify the investment in its Club Card.

The database and customer relationship management

CRM has been one of the business buzzwords of the last five years. It reflects the fact that marketing orientation must run through the entire enterprise. As organizations have come to recognize this, it has become clear that marketing is too important just to be the responsibility of the marketing 'department'; all parts of the business throughout the value chain, from suppliers to accounts and HR to our marketing intermediaries, have a role in promoting the organization and its products and services.

CRM attempts to reflect the reality of the customer experience. It is an old marketing chestnut, but it is nonetheless true that customers do not recognize the output of organizations as 'sales promotion' or 'advertising' or 'sales force' activity. All they see is an organization dealing with them as customers, potential customers (prospects) or lapsed customers, better or worse than another company.

Insight: Touching BMW

Research done for BMW by its award-winning below-the-line agency Archibald Ingall Stretton identified over 240 different ways in which a customer or prospect could come into contact with the BMW brand. Some of these are managed through communications planning, some can be controlled, perhaps through PR, some cannot be managed, for example word of mouth and day-to-day contact of customers with BMW drivers. The key output of this research was to provide BMW with a network analysis and allow them the opportunity to explore further the intensity and relevancy of these 'touchpoints' for customers.

Customer relationship management attempts to integrate an approach to customers that uses the information about them gleaned from multiple contact points to develop appropriate strategies to manage the customer experience to deliver a consistent customer experience that maximizes mutual value from the relationship. Gamble *et al.* (2001) define CRM as:

> *An enterprise wide commitment to identify your named individual customers and create a relationship between your company and these customers so long as that relationship is mutually beneficial.*

It is important to realize that for many organizations the word 'CRM' is inevitably attached to 'systems'. However, as you can see from the above definition it is not necessary for CRM to be IT based and indeed the design of CRM programmes, as with all strategic decisions in business, should involve the matching of resources to opportunities. That is, the system design should be appropriate to the resource base of the organization and its planned future growth. It is the IT systems that tend to cause most dissatisfaction. A survey by Gartner recently found that over 55 per cent of managers were dissatisfied with the results of the implementation of CRM systems in their business.

The idea should be that CRM aligns the business more effectively with customers' needs and wants and promotes solutions to customers more effectively and as a result more efficiently. Too often we seem to focus on efficiency without recognizing the impact that this has on effectiveness. If we raise expectations then we MUST deliver against these expectations.

In its optimum form, CRM integrates information sources, learns from this information and delivers a consistent targeted offer through multiple contact points. Customer information sits at the heart of this and will include data from the following:

◆ Websites
◆ Dealers
◆ Sales force
◆ Accounts

- Operation
- Fulfilment and response handling
- Call centres
- Partners
- Transaction data
- Marketing database.

Marketing research and the database

The MRS code of conduct that we shall look at in detail later specifically prohibits the use of market research to build databases.

Data collected by market research techniques must be aggregated and anonymous.

The research industry went to some lengths to ensure that it was exempt from the provisions of the 1998 Data Protection Act that would have severely compromised its role in social and economic research. We will look later at the way that anonymous research data can be used to enhance our understanding of the customers on our database. Despite this, it is clear that the use of databases can enhance the information that we hold on our prospects, and current and lapsed customers. The database can provide a sample frame of customers and marketing research can use this provided that the research design indicates that this is appropriate and free of bias.

Very often, however, the database does not adequately support pure marketing research simply because the sample that is available is only of existing customers, responders to past communications or lapsed customers. It probably does not include those who might be interested in a new product but have never responded or transacted with the company before. Given this, the uses of the database in helping the research function are limited.

Conversely the use of marketing research data overlaid on the database is becoming more common. Anonymous data can be linked at postcode level or other consumer characteristic to provide texture depth of understanding to information held on the database. Together the quality of management information is significantly enhanced.

Data protection and freedom of information

The United Kingdom has had data protection legislation since 1984. The current Data Protection Act which was passed in 1998 and came into force in 2000 was introduced in response to the 1995 European Union Directive on Data Protection. The Act regulates 'processing' of data; this covers data on any living person and there are separate rules for sensitive data, for example health, sexuality, religion, disabilities and so on. If you collect data on Halal meals then your data falls in this separate, more sensitive category. The Freedom of Information Act (2000) came into force on 1 January 2005. The Act regulates access to information held by public authorities.

The guiding principles of transparency and consent in the Data Protection Act are most relevant for marketing research professionals. Individuals must have a clear understanding of why their data is being captured and what it will be used for, and they must consent to its use and be given the opportunity to opt out of any later use of this data.

Opt-out is the standard at the moment in non-electronic communications. However, for e-mail and SMS the rule is opt in. We can use e-mail addresses for marketing provided that these names have been captured during a sale or negotiation towards a sale. These communications should always include an 'Unsubscribe' button.

The idea of asking all contacts to actively opt in to future use of their data is almost certain to become the standard and it is good practice now to ask individuals to actively opt in to the future use of their data.

There are three key terms to understand in the Act:

1   **Data controller** – the collector of data.

2   **Data processor** – the processor of the data. For example, Sainsbury is the collector of Nectar Card data and Loyalty Marketing Group is the processor.

3   **The data subject** – the individual on whom information is collected.

Every UK business that processes data must register with the Information Commissioner's offices; this can be done online at www.ICO.gov.uk. It costs £35 per year. As part of the process you must identify all uses to which the data will be put.

The current Act has eight key principles, you should familiarize yourself with these at some point in your course:

1st Principle – Data must processed fairly and lawfully.

2nd Principle – Data must be obtained only for specific and lawful purposes.

3rd Principle – Personal data must be adequate, relevant and not excessive in relation to the purposes for which it is processed.

4th Principle – Personal data must be accurate and where necessary, up to date, with every reasonable step taken to ensure this.

5th Principle – Personal data should not be kept for longer than is necessary.

6th Principle – Personal data shall be processed in accordance with the data subjects' rights. These include:

- Right to access – if an individual pays £10 within 30 days, a copy of the data held should be provided.

- Right to prevent data being used for direct marketing – direct marketing is communication by any means of advertising or marketing material communicated to particular individuals. Individuals can opt not to receive these.

- Right to prevent decisions being made on automated processing, for example automated decision on credit.

- Right to prevent processing that may cause damage or distress.

7th Principle – The data must be kept secure against accidental loss, destruction or damage.

8th Principle – Overseas transfer of data, should not be outside the European Economic Area (EU plus Norway, Iceland and Liechtenstein) unless consent is given. If data is exported, it must be to countries approved by the information commissioner. Hungary, Switzerland, New Zealand and Canada are the only ones that qualify at present. The United States has set up a system called 'safe harbour'. Under the safe harbour system US companies can self-certify as complying with EEA data rule. In the United States, 175 companies have signed up.

Penalties for non-compliance or contravention of the Act are fines of £5000 or more and damages.

Exemptions also exist for data processed for marketing research. Personal data for re-search can be reprocessed and data relating to longitudinal studies may be kept. Once data is anonymized, it can be kept indefinitely, and once personal identifiers are removed, subjects do not have the right to access data.

The advice is to take advice; enormous damage may be done through the negative public-ity surrounding breaches of the Data Protection Act.

There are a number of other relevant Acts but the Data Protection Act is the most onerous. You may need to consider the Telecommunications (Data Protection and Privacy) Regula-tions 1999 replaced on 11 December 2003 by the Privacy and Electronic Communications (EC Directive) Regulations 2003, which stipulate that it is unlawful to make unsolicited direct marketing calls to individuals who have indicated that they do not want to receive such calls via the Telephone Preference Service (TPS).

There is now also a Corporate TPS. To quote the TPS:

> The Corporate Telephone Preference Service (CTPS) is the central opt out register whereby corporate subscribers ... can register their wish not to receive unsolicited sales and marketing telephone calls to either all their organization's telephone num-bers, or to certain numbers. It is a legal requirement that companies do not make such calls to numbers registered on the CTPS.
>
> It takes 28 days for the registration to become fully effective.
>
> If you register any of your telephone numbers you need to be aware that you may not receive unsolicited telephone calls from other organizations which you and your colleagues may find useful and would be interested in receiving.
>
> For information on the Regulations which dictate this new legal requirement please visit Privacy and Electronic Communications (EC Directive) (Amendment) Regula-tions 2004 at www.hmso.gov.uk/si/si2004/20041039.htm (tpsonline.org 2006).

It also covers opt-out via the Fax Preference Service (FPS). These are the responsibility of the Director General of Telecommunications. There are codes of practice that relate to list and database practice; these amongst many other things, say that lists should be run against the latest Mail Preference Service (MPS) or baby MPS suppression files. They should comply with the Data Protection Act. They should not use selections from a data-base that is more than six months old. If data is to be used for a significantly different purpose than originally intended, then consumers must be informed.

Codes of practice and guidelines

These are self-regulatory codes developed by the professional bodies responsible for the regulation of the industry. These are not legally binding but do represent good practice, and members of the professional bodies must comply with the code of conduct. The MRS Code was updated in 2005 and is presented below. The full document is available online at: www.mrs.org.uk/standards/downloads/code2005.doc.

The ESOMAR code of conduct can be viewed at http://www.esomar.org/index.php/codes-guidelines.html. The MRS also publishes a range of guidelines on aspects of marketing research. The current list is as follows:

◆　Market research guidelines

◆　Best practice in Mystery Customer Research (also see new revised draft)

◆　Free Prize Draws Guidance Note

◆　Guidance Note: How to Apply the MRS Code of Conduct in Employee Research

◆　Guidelines for Research Among Children and Young People

◆　Internet Research Interim Guidance Note

◆　Qualitative Research Guidelines (also see new revised draft)

◆　Quantitative Data Collection Guidelines

◆　Questionnaire Design Guidelines

◆　The Responsibilities of Interviewers

◆　Legislative guidelines.

A basic guide to the Data Protection Act 1998

The Data Protection Act 1998 and Market Research: Guidance for MRS Members

◆　Market Research Processes and the Data Protection Act (DPA) 1998

◆　Draft guidelines

◆　Code of practice for conducting Market Research in town centres

◆　Draft Business to Business Guidelines

◆　Draft guidelines for collecting data for mixed or non-market research purposes

◆　Draft Mystery Shopping Guidelines

◆　Draft Observational Research Guidelines

◆　Draft Public Opinion Research Guidelines

◆　Draft Qualitative Research Guidelines

Source: MRS

The DMA code of practice

The DMA code of conduct is available at www.dma.org.uk. There are a range of codes that relate, for example, to SMS marketing and marketing to children. You should review these as part of your study at www.dma.org.uk/content/Pro-Code.asp.

The preference services

Preference services are suppression lists that enable consumers to stop receiving marketing communications via various media. Consumers register on the service, and companies must run and deduplicate their files against the suppression list. Information on these is available from the DMA at www.dma.org.uk (Figure 2.5). The e-mail preference service is a new service that is run out of DMA in the United States.

Preference services cover telephone, mail (there is a separate category for households expecting a baby), fax and e-mail.

The Mailing Preference Service allows consumers to register their wish not to receive unsolicited direct mail.

Baby MPS is a service which allows parents who have suffered a miscarriage or bereavement of a baby in the first weeks of life to register their wish not to receive baby-related mailings.

The Telephone Preference Service allows businesses and consumers to register their telephone numbers in order to not receive unsolicited sales and marketing calls.

The Fax Preference Service allows consumers and businesses to register their home or business fax number not to receive unsolicited sales and marketing faxes.

The Email Preference Service is a global service managed by the DMA in the States which allows you to register your email address so as not to receive unsolicited sales and marketing e-mail messages.

Since December 2003, UK law (EU Privacy and Electronic Comms Dir) changed so that EMPS only needs to be used for e-mail campaigns sent outside the EU.

Figure 2.5: DMA Services. *Source*: www.dma.org.uk

Code of Advertising Practice

This relates to broader communications and marketing and is available at:

http://www.asa.org.uk/asa/codes/cap_code

Summary

We started this unit by exploring the database and the range of applications it can support. We have explored the processes involved in setting up a database looking at the management issues and the process of capturing, verifying and enhancing data.

We saw that there were several types of data and that the data gathered varies from consumer to B2B markets. We looked at the process of gathering data on international customers and saw that this raises issues of consistency due to name and address formats. Data types include:

◆ Identification data

◆ Demographic data

◆ Financial data

◆ Lifestyle data

◆ Transactional data.

These fit into four categories:

◆ Behavioural data

◆ Volunteered data

◆ Profile data

◆ Attributed data.

We looked in detail at the process of setting up a database exploring each of the phases in turn. These were:

1 Business review

2 Data audit

3 Data strategy, specification and verification

4 Data verification

5 Hardware/software

6 Data capture, maintenance and enhancement

7 Management issues: should the database be run in-house/out-of-house?

8 Applications

9 Review.

We looked at data enhancement through lifestyle and geo-demographic systems.

We looked at the process of maintaining data and explored methods of deduplication.

We looked at analysis techniques including the use of OLAP tools, cluster regression and CHAID analysis.

Finally, we looked at the applications that the database can support. We saw that they could be described as:

◆ Planning

◆ Contacting customers

◆ Data processing

- Production
- Response handling
- Lead processing
- Campaign management
- Customer research
- Analysis.

The marketing applications of the database were summed as:

- Find
- Acquire
- Keep
- Cross-sell
- Up-sell
- Prevent inactivity
- Renew.

We looked at the role of CRM and the future of data-driven marketing.

Finally we looked at the range of legislation and codes relating to the management of data and research.

Bibliography

Antinou, T. (1997) Drilling or mining? Handling and analysis of data between now and the year 2000, *Marketing and Research Today*, 115–120

DeTienne, K. and Thompson, J. (1996) Database marketing and organizational learning theory: toward a research agenda. *Journal of Consumer Marketing*, 13, 5, 12 - 34

Downer (2002) in *The IDM Practitioners' Guide*, The IDM

Gamble, P., Stone, M. and Woodcock, N. (2001) *Up Close and Personal*, London: Kogan Page

Reichheld, F. (2001) T*he Loyalty Effect*, HBSP

Thomas, B. and Housden, M. (2003) *Direct Marketing in Practice*, Oxford: Elsevier Butterworth-Heinemann

Wilson, A. (2006) *Marketing Research: An Integrated Approach*, FT Prentice Hall, 2nd edition

Websites

Experian (2007) Experian Company Case Studies, www.experian.com

Siebel (2003) www.siebel.com.

Unit 3

The scope and nature of the research industry

Learning objectives

By the end of this unit you will be able to:

◆ Discuss the nature and structure of the market research industry.

◆ Explain the stages of the market research process.

◆ Evaluate a range of procedures and criteria used for selecting a market research supplier in domestic and international markets.

◆ Explain how best to liaise with the research agency on a day-to-day basis to leverage best levels of service, support and implementation and high quality information to support the business case development.

◆ Explain the stages involved in order to develop a full research proposal to fulfil the brief which support the information needs of different marketing projects.

◆ Evaluate the ethical and social responsibilities inherent in the market research task.

Table 3.1: Learning outcomes and knowledge and skills requirements

Learning outcomes	Knowledge and skills requirements
3.1 Discuss the nature and structure of the market research industry	Marketing research departments v. marketing research agencies Types of marketing research agency Scale of the industry Professional bodies and associations in the marketing research industry
3.2 Explain the stages of the market research process	Identification of problems and opportunities Formulation of research needs/the research brief Selection of research provider/the proposal Creation of research design Collection of secondary data Collection of primary data Analysis of data Preparation and presentation of research findings and recommendations
3.3 Evaluate a range of procedures and criteria used for selecting a market research supplier in domestic and international markets	Short-listing criteria The research proposal Supplier assessments (pitch) Selection criteria
3.4 Explain how best to liaise with the research agency on a day-to-day basis to leverage best levels of service, support and implementation and high quality information to support the business case development	Monitoring working arrangements using quality and service standards
3.5 Explain the stages involved in order to develop a full research proposal to fulfil the brief which support the information needs of different marketing projects	Content of proposal covering background, objectives, approach and method, reporting and presentation procedures, timing, personal CVs, related experience, contract details
3.6 Evaluate the ethical and social responsibilities inherent in the market research task	Need for goodwill, trust, professionalism, confidentiality Codes of marketing and social research practice (e.g. Market Research Society code of conduct) Responsibilities to respondents (Use of information/ protection of vulnerable groups such as children, etc.) Responsibilities to clients (transparency, data reporting, etc.)

Key definitions

The marketing research brief – Description of a research problem used to inform potential suppliers of solutions.

The proposal – A written and often an oral response to the research brief.

Qualitative research – An unstructured research approach using a small number of selected individuals to produce non-quantifiable insights into attitudes, behaviour, emotions and motivations.

Quantitative research – A structured research approach using a sample of the population designed to produce quantifiable data.

Primary research – Research carried out to meet a specific objective. It is new to the research world.

Secondary research – Published research or research carried out for another purpose.

Desk research – The collation of existing research results and data from published secondary sources for a different purpose (MRS, 2007).

Experimental research – Research measuring causality or the changing of one variable to observe the effect on another whilst other extraneous variables are kept constant.

Coding – The process of allocating codes to responses collected during fieldwork facilitating analysis of data (MRS, 2007).

Editing – Checking data for consistency, coherence and completeness before coding.

Exploratory research – Research intended to develop initial ideas or insights and to provide direction for any further research (Wilson, 2006).

Fieldwork – The collection of primary data from external sources by means of surveys, observation and experiment (MRS, 2007).

Group discussions/focus groups – A number of respondents gathered together to generate ideas through the discussion of, and reaction to, specific stimuli. Under the steerage of a moderator, focus groups are often used in exploratory work or when the subject matter involves social activities, habits and status (MRS, 2007).

Pilot – The pre-testing of a research design on a small scale prior to full roll out.

Longitudinal research – Data collection over time to examine trends.

Causal research – Research that examines whether one variable causes or determines the value of another variable (Wilson, 2006).

Descriptive research – Research studies that describe what is happening in a market without potentially explaining why it is happening (Wilson, 2006).

Observation research – A non-verbal means of obtaining primary data as an alternative or complement to questioning (MRS, 2007).

Study guide

This unit should take around two hours to complete.

Introduction

We now move on to the discipline of marketing research. In this unit we will look at the research planning process in detail. This will be important for you as it provides the frame-work for the next few sections of the workbook. We will introduce concepts here that will be explored in more detail in later units.

We will also explore the industry and the process of planning research and briefing re-searchers to carry out the process. This will be an important part of your course.

The senior examiner in a recent briefing to tutors told them to focus on the process of developing research briefs, responding to those briefs through the presentation of the proposal and then of the final report. This activity represents the day-to-day management of the research function in business and it forms an important part of your assessment in this module.

The brief and the proposal are very important. Even if the research is to be carried out in-house, a briefing document and proposal is required. They provide a fixed reference that all parties involved should sign off. For the commissioner of the research, it provides 'bullet proof' evidence that a certain date or budget was agreed on. In complex research studies, it keeps all parties on track and can help the process of project management.

The marketing research industry

The information industry has changed dramatically over the last 20 years in line with changes in business generally. The business has internationalized, and the major organi-zations that supply research and database services to the market are amongst the largest organizations in marketing services.

The industry has embraced new technology and whilst it is still possible to carry out re-search without the use of a computer, much of the drudgery has been taken out of the process.

The emergence of the Internet as a major channel and communications medium has meant that online research and research about online marketing is perhaps the fastest growing area.

In 2001 according to the organization responsible for the research industry in Europe, ESOMAR, US$15.9 billion was spent on marketing research worldwide; of this, US$1.7 billion was spent in the UK. By 2006 this had risen to $24.6 billion with $10.6 billion spent in Europe and $2.4 billion spent in the UK. ESOMAR estimates that the worldwide market research market grew by 4.0 per cent in 2006. Certain markets in Africa and the Middle East and Central and South America grew very quickly (Table 3.2).

More information and to purchase a full report containing this data and much more con-tact: www.esomar.org

Table 3.2: World market research turnover and growth rates by region 2003-6

Region	Turnover in million US$	Turnover in million US$*	Turnover in million US$	Real growth rate % (adj. for inflation)
	2003	2004	2006	2005/06
EU15	7,590	8,827	9,501	1.8
New member states	249	299	385	6.6
Other Europe	454	534	711	15.5
Total Europe	8,293	9,660	10,597	2.8
North America	7,137	7,853	8,884	3.4
Central and South America	720	830	1,121	11.3
Asia Pacific	2,526	2,863	3,530	6.6
Middle East & Africa	251	294	385	9.5
Total World	18,928	21,501	24618	4

* exchange rate fluctuations are eliminated, IMF exchange rates used

Source: ESOMAR Market Research Industry Survey 2007

Who carries out research?

Research and database information can be produced internally or externally and the management task can be carried out in-house or externally.

Internal research departments within companies may be carrying out research themselves and commissioning agencies to carry out work on their behalf. They will usually be responding to requests for research support from internal departments or working alongside the marketing team providing a range of research-based services.

Advertising and direct marketing agencies typically also carry out a significant amount of work within the planning function. This may involve a combination of research-based activity and increasingly database analysis to support the creation of effective communications activity. These agencies may be carrying out work themselves or commissioning a range of external suppliers. Alan Wilson (2006) identifies the types of organizations that exist to provide information and research services to the companies. These include:

List brokers – These are suppliers of lists of contacts for marketing purposes. They may include names and addresses, telephone numbers and e-mail addresses. Details of list owners and types are held by the DMA in the UK. You can see these at www.dma.org.uk.

Full service agencies – These are agencies that provide a full range of research services, for example, TNS.

Specialist service agencies – Specialize in certain types of research, e.g. international or online research.

Field agencies – Specialize in the delivery of fieldwork and the administration of questionnaires.

Data analysis companies – Specialize in the analysis of data.

Consultants – These are independent consultants who may offer a range of services.

Other suppliers into the industry include database bureaux who may host an external database for a company.

Table 3.3: Leading UK research companies by turnover 2004

COMPANY	2004 (£'000)	2004 vs. 2003 (%)	Total ranking	Domestic ranking	International ranking
TNS plc	161.4	1.2	1	1	1
NOP World	80.3	5.1	2	2	3
Synovate	51.9	11.5	3	6	2
Ipsos (UK) Ltd	49.4	5.1	4	4	5
MORI (Market & Opinion Research International)	44.2	12.2	5	3	11
Information Resources	35.2	4.6	6	5	15
HI Europe	23.5	6.8	7	8	4
Incepta Marketing Intelligence	20.0	2.0	8	7	7
GfK Martin Hamblin	15.5	−10.9	9	13	6
ORC International	12.5	0.1	10	9	12
Marketing Sciences	7.7	5.1	11	14	13
Total	501.6	5.4			

Source: BMRB

Table 3.4: Top 15 global research companies 2006

Ranking 2006	Ranking 2005	Company	Country
1	1	The Nielsen Company	USA
2	3	IMS Health Inc	USA
3	2	Talyor Nelson Sofres Plc	UK
4	5	The Kantar Group	UK
5	4	GfK AG	Germany
6	6	Ipsos Group SA	France
7	8	Synovate	UK
8	7	IRI	USA
9	9	Westet Inc	USA
10	10	Arbitron Inc	USA
11	11	INTAGE Inc	Japan
12	14	JD Power and Associates	USA
13	12	Harris Interactive Inc	USA
14	13	Maritz Research	USA
15	16	The NFD Group Inc	USA

Source: ESOMAR 2006

For information and to buy a copy of the ESOMAR Global Market Research Report go to www.ESOMAR.org. This data is provided by ESOMAR, an invaluable resource for the market researcher. You should visit the website and save it in your favourites.

ESOMAR promote their mission as:

> *To promote the use of opinion and market research for improving decision-making in business and society worldwide. Founded in 1948, ESOMAR unites 4000 members in 100 countries, both clients and providers of opinion and marketing research. Members can also be found in advertising and media agencies, universities and business schools, as well as in public authorities and institutions.*

The suppliers of research service in the UK can be identified via the MRS's *Research Buyers Guide* which is available online or in print format. ESOMAR also provides a directory of its members. They are both excellent at identifying potential agencies and their relevant skills base.

The *Research Buyer's Guide* of the MRS lists the following for all its members:

◆ Address and telephone number

◆ Turnover (Bands)

◆ Services (all and specialities)

◆ Key executives/All full members

◆ Brief description

◆ IQCS membership

◆ Date formed

◆ Ownership.

Activity 3.1

Go to www.MRS.org.uk and look at the *Research Buyer's Guide*. Try to find companies that specialise in the following sectors:

◆ Food and drink

◆ Transportation

◆ Business to business.

Look also for the following methodologies:

◆ Pan European studies

◆ Ethnography

◆ Online qualitative research

These companies are carrying out a variety of research techniques (Table 3.5). The table shows the split between techniques. Do not worry if you do not understand all the terms – you will by the end of this book!

Table 3.5: Per cent research turnover by method 2006

Type of research	%
Face-to-face interviews	12
Telephone interviews	19
Postal	4
Online	16
Other quantitative	32
Total quantitative	83
Groups	10
In-depth interviews	2
Other qualitative	2
Total qualitative	14

Source: ESOMAR (2007)

Professional bodies and institutes

There are a range of bodies that support the profession in the United Kingdom. These are divided between the professional institutes and the professional associations. The main difference is that the institutes support the individuals in the industry while the association supports the industry in the economy.

In the UK, the institutes that support the market researcher and information professional include:

◆ The **CIM** – www.cim.co.uk

◆ The **MRS** – www.mrs.org.uk

◆ The **IDM** – www.theidm.com.

The associations that support the marketing research and information industry include:

◆ The **British Market Research Organization** (BMRA) – www.bmra.org.uk. (the BMRA merged with the Market Research Society in 2006 and their services are now consolidated within the MRS).

◆ The **Direct Marketing Association** (DMA) – www.dma.org.uk.

These national institutes and associations are linked to regional and world representative bodies. For example, the MRS is linked to ESOMAR or the World Association of Opinion and Marketing Research Professionals (WAPOR).

The origins of ESOMAR were in Europe. It was founded in 1948 as the European Society for Opinion and Marketing Research. Its links with WAPOR mean it represents over 4000 members in 100 countries.

ESOMAR can be found at www.esomar.org and WAPOR at www.unl.edu/WAPOR. Both sites are well worth visiting.

The DMA is linked to FEDMA, the Federation of European Direct Marketing. FEDMA can be found at www.fedma.org.

Most of the national bodies have a links page through to their international counterparts.

Activity 3.2

Review the Direct Marketing Association's site at www.dma.org.uk. What does it do that its European counterpart FEDMA www.FEDMA.org does not do?

Do the same for the MRS and ESOMAR www.mrs.org.uk and www.esomar.org.

The marketing research process

The planning process for marketing is important (Table 3.6). Research costs money and takes time, and a planned approach to the process can save both.

Table: 3.6: The marketing research process

1   Identify the problem or opportunity
  * Exploratory research

2   Issue a research brief
  * Exploratory research

3   Develop a proposal and research design

4   Select agency
  * Exploratory research

5   Secondary data
  * Internal
  * External

6   Primary data
  * Qualitative
  * Quantitative

7   Piloting and data capture; fieldwork

8   Data input, coding and editing

9   Analysis

10   Results and findings

11   Report presentation

12   Feedback

13   Business decision

The process may appear complicated but the degree of complexity is dependent on the nature of the research task. Research problems may be solved at the exploratory or internal research phase and a decision may result from a simple database enquiry. For example, 'how many of our customers were repeat buyers last year?' Other problems may demand more complex solutions and may involve the use of multiple external partners to deliver.

Let us look at each stage of the process.

Review the business situation

We start the process with a review of the current business position. Restating the values and mission of the business, and identifying markets served and our unique selling proposition should help to focus the research process on the broader goals of the business. It usually helps to state the marketing objectives of the business and summarize the current marketing plan, which should provide the underpinning for all activity.

Marketing decisions need to be made in response to a constantly changing business environment and research may be needed to inform these decisions.

Activity 3.3

You are a marketing manager for a major whisky manufacturer. Whisky sales are stagnant and you are looking at the success of spirits-based drinks like Reef and Breezer. You have been asked to look at the development of a whisky-based drink to target a younger market. What information would you need to carry out this project?

The review of the business environment is an ongoing process and research requirements may reflect the dynamic nature of this environment – for example, customers' reaction to a competitor's new product. Or, it may reflect the planned development of the business as expressed in the marketing plan – for example, the international launch of a product range.

The process of environmental scanning may be the responsibility of the research department and the issue of sector or competitive briefings either face to face or through a corporate intranet may be part of this process. The vital thing is that the key decision-makers are kept informed of changes and are able to make intelligent decisions. The business case needs to be established as resources within the marketing function are always under pressure. We need to ensure that the research proposed is fully informed by the business situation and that the relative costs and benefits are weighed up before going ahead.

Defining the issues or problem

Defining the problem, despite appearances, is not easy. Problems can generally be solved in many ways. The problem definition needs to reflect the organization's resources, or be expressed in a way that clearly identifies the opportunity that is being looked at. Sometimes, a view of the problem for a pressured executive may not actually be the real issue. The research company or internal research department that is asked to review marketing communications activity may find that there are particular political issues with the current agency or that the brand is poorly managed or that the pricing strategy is wrong.

Very often we have to carry out informal or exploratory research to identify and define the research question we are trying to answer. Poor research questions or problem definition can lead to expensive and unnecessary work being carried out.

Research problems and objective setting

Being able to define a problem and set objectives in an appropriate way is very important. Often managers appear to want the answer to the meaning of life by 5.00 p.m. Understanding the business, so as to be able to isolate and define a problem, is a skill that comes with experience. For example, the ill-informed manager may set an objective to determine 'why are our sales falling?' while the experienced manager might say 'what are the perceptions of our service standards against our key competitors?' He has already limited the research to a narrow problem area and researchers have a much clearer idea of the purpose to which the research will be put. It may be that the researcher has to carry out this refining and defining process but it can be helped by good communication and understanding at this stage.

Carry out exploratory research

This stage, as outlined above, is designed to clarify the research problem, it is often an ongoing process especially as the project develops in the early stages. It is largely informal and may involve a range of techniques. It should involve discussions with those who are involved with the problem and its solution. It may involve a review of the trade press and simple scanning of internal documents and resources. The aim is to inform the process and to become 'immersed' in the problem and its potential solutions.

Even at this stage the researcher may be thinking ahead about methods that could be used to deliver the information required. The key thing is to uncover the real purpose of the research and, possibly, the constraints in terms of time and budget that may affect the process. We also need, at this stage, to think about the value of the research. There is little point in spending more on research than the profit to be gained by making a right decision, or the cost of making a wrong decision.

Remember research will not eliminate risk entirely but may reduce it to acceptable levels. An understanding of the commercial constraints of carrying out research may be gained through intuition or experience but it can also be worked out more scientifically.

If research is required to justify packaging redesign, then we can estimate the improved sales of such a move and offset the cost of research against this. This objective-and-task approach to setting research budgets is the best way of managing research budgets. However, it is not always possible to carry out this process accurately.

If the cost of a research project to determine between two product flavours was £25,000, and the research-based launch generated incremental profits of £40,000, then clearly, the research is worthwhile. It should always be possible to estimate the likely impact on a project if it is done with or without research and this can help in determining whether the research should be done and the extent of that research.

Previous research

As part of this process, previously carried out research should be reviewed to see if the problem has been dealt with elsewhere. It may be that the solution lies in work that has been done in other departments. For example, work to improve the navigation of the website may have been done in the IT department. Access to previously commissioned work may be through the intranet or through the company library. Or it may be that individual managers have commissioned research which has not been distributed widely through the organization.

Internal research

Internal research will involve the use of the MkIS or marketing decision support system and the marketing or other operational databases. It may be that the problem, as we said, can be solved at this stage. Whatever, it is worth spending time now on internal records to, maybe, solve the problem or help to define it. For example, a problem that involves finding out the average age of a company's existing customers may be solved through a simple interrogation of the customer database.

Redefine the problem

The output of this stage is a clear statement of the research problem that is agreed by all parties. After this, a brief can be written.

The marketing research brief, short listing and proposal

These sections are covered in more detail below. However, a brief should be written for all projects even if the research is to be carried out in-house. The proposal written to the brief will become the contract for the research when it is accepted, and is equally important.

Research design

In this part of the process, we start thinking about the type of research methods we might employ to solve the particular problem we have identified. At this stage, we will introduce the terms. Later we will drill down into more detail.

Wilson identifies three types of marketing research. These are:

◆ Exploratory

◆ Conclusive – descriptive research

◆ Conclusive – causal research.

Whilst Wilson tells us that these are not mutually exclusive, they represent a research continuum from purely descriptive to purely causal.

◆ **Exploratory research** is intended to develop initial ideas or insights and to provide direction for further research.

◆ **Conclusive research** covers all other research that is aimed at evaluating alternative courses of action or measuring and monitoring the organization's performance.

◆ **Conclusive descriptive research** provides answers to the who, what, where, when and how of marketing research. It explains what is happening, but not why. Descriptive research may be cross-sectional, that is involving data collection at a single point of time. Or, it may be longitudinal involving data collection over time to examine trends.

◆ **Conclusive causal research** tells us if one variable is related to another. That is, if one variable causes or determines the value of another. For example, drinks and ice cream companies look at the influence of temperature on product sales. A simpler more common approach would be to look at the effect of different creative executions on response rates. This latter example is an example of experimental research or the changing of one variable to observe the effect on another whilst other extraneous variables are kept constant.

Secondary or desk research

Desk or secondary research is information that has already been gathered for some other purpose. It may be held within the organization or by other organizations. It is called desk research because it is usually accessible from a desk via the intranet or online or in hard copy. This is dealt with in detail in the next section.

In the research plan, desk research is carried out before primary research. This is because it is generally cheaper. It may solve the problem without any need for expensive primary work. Typically we move from internal sources to external sources exhausting the most cost-effective solutions before moving to more expensive and time-consuming secondary sources.

Primary research

Primary research is research carried out to meet a specific objective. It is 'new to the world research'. Primary research is the common currency of marketing research. It is what most of us have come across either through telephone research, or face-to-face interviews or increasingly through online research.

Primary research is may be qualitative or quantitative.

Qualitative research

> **Qualitative research** – a body of research techniques which seeks insights through loosely structured, mainly verbal data rather than measurements. Analysis is interpretative, subjective, impressionistic and diagnostic. (MRS 2007)

Qualitative research describes research that cannot be quantified or subjected to quantitative analysis. It typically uses small sample sizes and is designed to produce a depth of understanding, context and insight.

It helps to uncover the motivation behind the behaviour rather than to identify the behaviour itself. It seeks to get under the skin of respondents, uncovering their deeper feelings. It is essentially subjective but is a highly developed and important research methodology.

Quantitative research

> **Quantitative research** – research which seeks to make measurements as distinct from qualitative research. (MRS 2007)

Quantitative is the opposite of qualitative in that it is statistically verifiable. It provides answers to the questions 'who' and 'how many' rather than the depth of insight as to why. It uses a structured approach to problem-solving using a sample of the population to make statistically based assumptions about the behaviour of the population as a whole.

Data capture

Both qualitative and quantitative work require some form of data collection. In qualitative work, this usually involves the creation of a topic guide, which helps the researcher to ensure that all the areas intended to be covered have been dealt with. The data capture mechanism is usually an electronic recording either digitally or via audio or videotape.

Quantitative research is usually gathered and recorded via questionnaire. This can be delivered via a number of different media including face-to-face, telephone, mail or online.

The pilot

All primary research should be piloted or tested to see that the data collection methods are sound. This may be difficult with some forms of qualitative work but a basic run-through is very important. Pilots will help with the structure and sequencing of questions and may identify areas of questioning that have not been considered. It ensures that the data collection device is effective and efficient.

Fieldwork

Fieldwork is the generic term given to the collection of primary data. It may cover the collection of a range of data. The administration of a major quantitative study may involve serious logistical considerations whilst qualitative work may involve highly qualified and skilled researchers.

The management of fieldwork is often given to specialist field managers or fieldwork agencies. The process is very important as the failure to adhere to methodology at this stage may compromise the entire project.

Data input, coding and editing

Data that is gathered from respondents must be recorded and edited to produce a data set that is capable of being analysed. In qualitative work, this may mean producing a transcript of the interview. In quantitative work, it means creating a data set that the computer can work with. This is covered in detail later on.

All potential responses must be given a different code to enable analysis. Data is checked for completeness and consistency, and if there are significant problems the respondent may be called back to check details.

Often today, data is input straight into the computer via systems known as CATI, CAPI and CAWI. These are:

◆ CATI – Computer-aided telephone interviewing

◆ CAPI – Computer-aided personal interviewing

◆ CAWI – Computer-aided web interviewing.

Data analysis

Data is analysed via the computer to produce a range of results.

Results, findings and recommendations

A marketing decision should result from the results of the research. Results should be presented clearly in a way that focuses on the problem to be solved. It is easy with today's statistical packages to produce hundreds of tables to a high degree of statistical sophistication. Results must be presented in a way that is accessible to the audience and that clearly presents the solution to the problem posed.

Report/presentation

Presentation of the results will usually be in the form of a written report and this may be supported by an oral presentation. The data will need to be presented but this should be in the appendices. The body of the report remains solutions-focused.

Business decision

The output should be marketing decisions that are made at reduced risk and a feedback loop should exist to the business situation.

The marketing research brief

We will now look in more detail at the marketing research brief. The briefing document is perhaps the most important stage of the research process. As the old aphorism states 'be careful what you ask for, you may get it'. A tight brief is vital to the management of the marketing research process. It provides a focus for discussion and a guiding hand through the project.

Many companies see the briefing process as part of an almost gladiatorial trial of strength where a brief is issued, limited information is given, and the resulting proposals are torn to bits in the arena of the pitch. The justification is that ideas are tested in the heat of the moment and that if an agency cannot justify an approach under fire, they are unlikely to be effective. The lack of detail is seen as allowing the agency to interpret and explore ideas. Some research briefs are given on one side of a page of A4. This may be sufficient but is almost certainly inadequate for complex multifaceted research tasks. Equally some companies go the other way, even specifying the colour and weight of paper for the final presentation. This may be overkill. On the other side, some agencies receive a brief as Drayton Bird (2007) says 'rather like a baby bird waiting to be fed by its mother, passively, humbly and gratefully'.

Both approaches are wrong. The best marketing solutions come through cooperation and active involvement. Agencies need the right information in order to be able to produce a suitable proposal. If there are issues over confidentiality, then, confidentiality agreements can be signed before the brief is issued. Members of the MRS are obliged to comply with the code of conduct that ensures client confidentiality. But the agency needs the tools to do the job – in this case, information.

The development of the brief should be a team activity. The structure is outlined below:

◆ **Identification details** – Should include the title, date, contact names and details.

◆ **Current business position** – Should detail the nature and scope of the business, key markets served, key competitors and future direction.

- ◆ **Marketing and business objectives** – Should be laid down and distinguished between.

- ◆ **Research objectives** – Will almost certainly differ from marketing objectives but are informed by them. For example, the marketing objectives may be to enter a new market while the research objectives may be to identify the product attributes that appeal most to potential customers.

- ◆ **How the results will be used** – The overall purpose and context for the research needs to be specified. How will the research be used and what other decisions might it inform in the future?

- ◆ **Outline methodology** – This is a difficult area but in discussing the problem, research methods may have been discussed. Certainly, where there is expertise in the briefing team the research methodology may have been discussed in detail. There is no danger in allowing the proposing agency to have access to these views. Certainly the brief should include details on whether a qualitative or quantitative approach is required. Also outline question areas could be given.

- ◆ **Sample details** – The details of the group of interest should be indicated. If the sample is to include businesses over a certain size, then the agency should be told to avoid wasting their time.

- ◆ **Previous research** – Previously commissioned work that is relevant to the current study may be outlined or made available to the agency pitching for the business.

- ◆ **Timings** – It is important that a detailed timetable of activity is included. This should cover time for questions, and details of the formal date and time for the presentation to take place if this is required.

- ◆ **Budget** – A tricky area but generally it is advisable to give some indication of the budget that is available for the project.

- ◆ **Deliverables** – How will the results be presented and when? Will there be a formal debriefing presentation? How many copies of reports will be needed?

- ◆ **Terms and conditions** – Confidentiality and so on.

- ◆ **Key personnel names** – And details of all key staff involved in the project.

Briefing

(Note: This is a cut-down brief presented to ensure client confidentiality)

Usage and attitudes in the ambient ready meals market (ARMs)

Purpose of the research to establish usage and attitudes to the consumption of ambient ready meals in the five EU markets (specified elsewhere).

Background to the company

Description of the company

Ownership, turnover, brands, ambient ready meal brands

Market size and market share data, trend's volume and value's competition

Background to the problem

Falling retail share, seek to stabilize market share through refined mix

Research objectives

Why are ARMs bought?

When are they used?

Who prepares them?

On what occasions?

Perception of quality relative to other RM categories

Perception of quality relative to competitors

Attitudes to price

Attitudes to advertising

Methods

Qualitative

Focus groups in key target audiences

Quantitative

Around 1500 housewives in each market, representative of households, quota sample

Question areas built out of the qualitative study

Brands bought, brands recognized, consumption occasion, attitudes to ARMs and other RM categories

We would like your advice on this aspect of research design and implementation

Timing

Proposal: 2 April

Presentation: week commencing 12 April

Commission: 4 May

Report: early July

Budget

In the region of £25,000

Report to

Brand manager

Marketing research manager

Marketing director.

Short listing

Once the brief is written and agreed, it should be sent to a short list of agencies. The short list generally should be no longer than four. Occasionally, more than four agencies are asked to pitch. It is courteous to let the agencies know how many other companies they are up against. It is unlikely that if they value their work that they will refuse to pitch.

The MRS code of conduct covers the duties and responsibilities of agencies and clients and recommends that four agencies are used. It also covers the issue of ownership of the work on the proposal, which can be significant.

The proposal

Once the brief has been received the agencies will work to create a proposal. This may take some time and the costs involved can be high. This explains the need for a sense of responsibility on the company or department issuing the brief.

The proposal should be presented in a written format and on time. A formal presentation may accompany the proposal. It is more effective that the proposal should be seen before any formal face-to-face presentation in order for it to be assessed and questions framed.

These questions may be sent to the agency before the formal meeting. A proposal may form the final contract for a project and as such can include contract details and terms and conditions as an appendix.

The proposal is a marketing tool for the research agency and the use of client testimonials and relevant past contracts is normal. It goes without saying that presentation, spelling and grammar should be faultless.

Contents of the research proposal

- Background
    - A clear statement of the business
    - The background to the research and other supporting insight
- Objectives
- Approach and method
    - Secondary Internal
    - Sources
    - Secondary external
    - Sources
- Primary
    - Sampling and recruitment
    - Qualitative
    - Quantitative
- Data analysis techniques
- Reporting and presentation procedures
- Timing
- Fees
    - By activity
- Personal CVs
- Related experience and references
- Contract details

Refining the proposal

Creating the proposal is a task that involves communication between client and the researcher. This may involve a face to face meeting. The aim is to refine the brief and to allow the researcher to produce an effective proposal.

Questions that may be asked or information requested include:

◆ Background data on market conditions and PEST factors

◆ Position of the brand

◆ Customers: awareness, attitude and behaviour of customers

◆ Competitor activity

◆ Company objectives, plans and capabilities

◆ Previous marketing initiatives – lessons from success or failure, examples

◆ Access to past research or information held on the database

◆ Nature of proposed products or services (if applicable)

◆ The range and influence of all stakeholders in the project

◆ Identify what current information is held

◆ What will the information be used for

◆ What methodologies and analysis would be required

◆ Presentation requirements, formal, oral, copies of documents, format

◆ Who will see the research and be present at the presentation

◆ Clarification of budget and deadlines.

Once the proposal is received, short-listed agencies will normally present the proposal to the client and a decision is made to appoint. Typcally the proposal will form the basis of the contract between the client and the appointed agency.

Selecting the agency

The project could, of course, be carried out in-house but the necessary capacity, skills, and specialist facilities may not be available. Equally an internal department may not be sufficiently removed from the problem to consider it objectively. The issue of political independence may also emerge. Finally it is not always cheaper to use an internal department. Typically there is an internal recharge made and this may be more than using the services of an efficient external agency.

In-house or out-of-house

In-house has a range of advantages:

◆ Control of the research process rests with those who commissioned the work.

◆ Awareness of the market or sector dynamics.

◆ Knowledge of both methodology and results resides within the organization of the cumulative knowledge.

◆ Costs – it may be cheaper to manage the tasks in-house.

◆ Timing – it may be quicker to produce results.

Disadvantages include:

◆ Lack of skills or methodological expertise.

◆ Inability to provide true national or international coverage.

◆ Bias in terms of interpreting the result from a predetermined point of view.

Advantages of using an agency include:

◆ Tighter cost control may be possible.

◆ Penalty clauses in contracts can protect the commissioning party.

◆ MRS code of conduct or other industry quality control standards will ensure the integrity of data.

◆ There is no political element to the research.

Disadvantages:

◆ Conflict of interest with other clients.

◆ Lack of industry expertise.

◆ Allocation of junior staff to smaller projects.

Criteria that may be used when selecting an external agency:

◆ Advice from colleagues

◆ Past experience

◆ Seen their work in the trade press

◆ Seen a credentials publication

◆ Size of the business

◆ Reputation

◆ Sector-specific skills

◆ Industry award winners

◆ Response to marketing activity

◆ Web searches

◆ They are local to us

◆ Recommendation from consultants or business advisors, for example, Business Link

◆ Trade body research.

So how do we finally select the agency?

Wilson (2006) identifies a checklist of seven points:

1 The agency's ability to understand the brief and translate it into a comprehensive proposal.

2 The compatibility of agency and client teams. Can we work with them?

3 The evidence of innovation in the proposal. Has the agency added value?

4 Evidence of understanding of the market and the problem facing the organization.

5 Sound methodology.

6 Meeting budget and time scales.

7 Relevant experience.

To this we can add relevant professional body memberships.

Managing the agency relationship

Baker and Mouncey (2003) wrote the following about the problems that research companies have in adding real value to the relationship with their clients. They describe this as an issue faced by many research businesses locked as they say in a 'cultural prison'.

We have been struck by how repetitive some of the messages have been and found ourselves asking why so little change has followed. We would offer the view that the industry has not moved quickly enough and appears to have been struck by a level of inertia characteristic of 'cultural prisoners' – those who find themselves doing things the way they've always been done simply because that's the way they've always been done. Are there any 'cultural architects' within the industry in a position to move now to build a brighter future?

They go on to say that good researchers should adhere to the following rules to enhance the relationship with their clients:

◆ Get very involved with the marketing team and understand their problems.

◆ Anticipate research opportunities.

◆ Constantly develop research tools which relate to the commercial issues your company and its clients face.

◆ Deliver your research more effectively and more efficiently.

◆ Investigate opportunities to deliver research 'online', especially continuous research.

◆ Encourage informal contact with users.

◆ Take all opportunities to 'educate' senior management on the actual and potential value of research to the business.

◆ Be intellectually attuned to your key clients' needs.

◆ Be sensitive to broad user needs, including the political aspect of commissioning of research and applications in decision-making.

◆ Create a trusting and open relationship with users.

◆ Be self-critical, reflective but value your contribution.

It goes without saying that this is the type of relationship that clients should be looking for in a research company. The recruitment of any agency needs to be based on sound relationships at both the business and personal level. Mutual respect, concern and understanding are the cornerstones of good agency–client relations and the best people will go out of their way to ensure that the job is done to the clients' specifications.

Relationships based solely on power games or solely on price and the budget are unlikely to live for a long time. Remember both parties in any deal have to make money.

Recruiting international agencies today is straightforward, but there are a range of additional complexities involved.

Proctor (2005) and Wilson (2006) suggest different approaches to carry out international research.

1   Using own staff or importing agents:

Problems here may be due to lack of impartiality and lack of skills.

2   Using overseas agencies or a consortium of agencies:

Selection may be difficult but they should possess knowledge of their home markets. Problems here include variability between agencies.

3   Using a UK-based firm supported by locally-based researchers:

This offers few advantages over 2.

4   Using a multinational agency:

Most major agencies in the UK have overseas offices or a network of associate agencies operating overseas. In selecting one of these, the problems of international research are potentially reduced as the agency will need to manage an appropriate methodology to meet the objectives of the study.

They will need to ensure that language and cultural differences are recognized and built into research design. The use of back translation of questionnaires and careful piloting is crucial to ensuring comparability in these areas.

They will need to ensure that the research covers similar product use and definition. For example, candied fruits are classified as confectionery products in parts of SE Asia, this may impact on a market sizing study for Cadbury, for example.

They also need to ensure that proposed methodologies are appropriate for each market. For example, online research in some regions is easier than in others.

Working together

Regular face to face meetings and formal interim reports may be useful during the project but extranets and dispersed project management software can help with complex multinational projects.

Ethics, regulation and codes of practice in market research

This section contains a lot of detail which is important in managing the reputation of the research industry and the rights of individual respondents.

The 'data' industry has grown rapidly as the technology that is available to capture, store, analyse and exchange data has improved. The amount of data held on individuals is incredible and this raises many issues. The data has value. It has personal and possibly material value to the individual, and commercial value to the company that has acquired it. It also has a range of costs associated with its capture and storage. It is therefore important that companies manage the data effectively and do not betray the trust placed in them by individuals who may have given up very sensitive information. The amount of data captured will only increase. Location information of users can be captured by 3G mobile phones and this can be used to target customers with messages for local retail stores.

In Chapter 2 we explored some of the regulations relating to data. Here we are going to look in more detail at those relating to research.

Wilson (2006) points out that ethics in market research are the moral guidelines that govern the conduct of behaviour in the marketing research industry. He says that the industry is dependent on:

◆ **Goodwill of respondents** – They have to be willing to carry out research and give up information.

◆ **Trust** – Underpins all relationships in the industry. Respondents have to trust researchers to handle their data in an ethical manner; clients trust researchers to carry out research properly.

◆ **Professionalism** – Data must be used in a professional manner.

◆ **Confidentiality** – Data must be kept confidential and anonymous, and not disclosed to third parties. The right to privacy is enshrined in the Human Rights Act.

The codes of conduct we looked at in the last chapter are very important to ensure the credibility and integrity of the industry.

The basic principles of the code specify that:

◆ Market researchers will conform to all relevant national and international laws.

◆ Market researchers will behave ethically and will not do anything which might damage the reputation of market research.

◆ Market researchers will take special care when carrying out research among children and other vulnerable groups of the population.

◆ Respondents' cooperation is voluntary and must be based on adequate, and not misleading, information about the general purpose and nature of the project when their agreement to participate is being obtained and all such statements must be honoured.

◆ The rights of respondents as private individuals will be respected by market researchers and they will not be harmed or disadvantaged as the result of cooperating in a market research project.

◆ Market researchers will never allow personal data they collect in a market research project to be used for any purpose other than market research.

◆ Market researchers will ensure that projects and activities are designed, carried out, reported and documented accurately, transparently, objectively and to appropriate quality.

◆ Market researchers will conform to the accepted principles of fair competition.

Source: MRS 2008

Without these assurances the industry may come under significant pressure. Already we are seeing that levels of opt-out on TPS and the electoral register are growing significantly and research response rates in certain media are suffering. Trust between researchers and respondents is key and cannot be compromised.

Summary

In this unit we looked at the research planning process, through the briefing process and the response to the brief through the creating of the research proposal.

We saw that the definition of the research problem is enabled through internal and exploratory research. The use of research should be justified where possible by the cost of making a poor marketing decision or the profit to be made from a better marketing decision.

We saw that the efficient solution of problems through research means that we should start with the cheapest sources of information, that is secondary or desk research. If this does not produce the required information, then we move to primary work.

We outlined the different types of marketing research and looked at qualitative and quantitative work. We saw that qualitative work should precede and inform the development of quantitative methodology. We looked in detail at the difference between qualitative and quantitative work.

We went on to look in detail at the briefing process and looked at each stage in turn.

◆ Identification details

◆ Current business position

◆ Marketing and business objectives should be set out and distinguished between

◆ Research objectives

◆ How the results will be used?

◆ Outline methodology

◆ Sample details

◆ Previous research

◆ Timings

◆ Budget

◆ Deliverables

◆ Terms and conditions

◆ Key personnel.

We saw that the brief was an important document and that the proposal which is delivered by the short-listed agencies, ultimately, will become the contract for the research programme.

We looked at the process of producing a proposal and how we should select the agency.

◆ Identification data

◆ Situation analysis

◆ Research objectives

◆ Methodology and rationale

- Sample
- Fieldwork
- Questionnaire/topic guide
- Data handling and processing
- Reporting
- Timetable
- Costs
- CVs of key staff
- Supporting evidence
- Contract details.

We saw that the final selection of the agency was based on a range of criteria including:

- The agency's ability to understand the brief and translate it into a comprehensive proposal.
- The compatibility of agency and client teams. Can we work with them?
- The evidence of innovation in the proposal. Has the agency added value?
- Evidence of understanding of the market and the problem facing the organization.
- Sound methodology.
- Meeting budget and time scales.
- Relevant experience.
- Relevant professional body memberships.

We looked at the management of international projects. Finally we revisited the role of ethics and the ICC/ESOMAR, MRS code of conduct

Bibliogrpahy

Baker, S. and Mouncey, P. (2003) The market researcher's manifesto, *International Journal of Marketing Research* 45 (4)

Crouch, S. and Housden, M. (2003) *Marketing Research for Managers*, Oxford: Elsevier Butterworth-Heinemann, 3rd edition

Proctor, T. (2005) *Essentials of Marketing Research*, FT Prentice Hall, 4th edition

Wilson, A. (2006) *Marketing Research: An Integrated Approach*, FT Prentice Hall, 2nd edition

Websites

Drayton Bird (2007) www.draytonbird.com

MRS (2008) www.mrs.org

Unit 4 Secondary data

Learning objectives

On completing this unit you will be able to:

◆ Discuss the uses, benefits and limitations of secondary data.

Table 4.1: Learning outcomes and knowledge and skills requirements

Learning outcomes	Knowledge and skills requirements
4.1 Discuss the uses, benefits and limitations of secondary data	Benefits of secondary data
	Limitations of secondary data
	Sources of secondary data
	Integrating secondary data with primary data

Key definitions

External data – Data that is held by external organizations.

Internet – An international, open access, network of computers.

World Wide Web – A system of interlinked hypertext documents that are accessed via the Internet, and which can be viewed and navigated using a web browser.

Intranet – A closed private company network based on web technology.

Extranet – A private company network, like an intranet, but to which customers, suppliers and other external stakeholders may be given access.

Search engines – Internet-based tools for searching for Uniform Resource Location (URL) or web addresses.

Newsgroups – Web-based notice board services.

Chat rooms – Locations on the Internet enabling web-based text or video-based real time interaction.

ISP – Internet service provider.

Study guide

This unit should take you around two hours to complete. You will need to explore online services, so make sure that you have access to the Internet.

Introduction

Secondary desk research is an important part of the researcher's armoury. In the last unit, we saw that the key goal of marketing research is to provide effective solutions efficiently. The use of desk research can ensure this. In the planning process, it precedes primary work. This is because it generally can be acquired at lower cost and can be obtained far more quickly. The key thing for the researcher is knowing where and how to look, and how to judge the quality of this work. In the IT age, there are a vast range of sources available to the researcher; some are more reliable than others.

What is secondary or desk research?

The MRS (2007) defines desk research as:

The collation of existing research results and data from published secondary sources for a specific, often unrelated, project.

Crouch and Housden (2003) define secondary desk research as:

Data that has already been published by someone else, at some other time period, usually for some other reason than the present researcher has in mind. The researcher is therefore a secondary user of already existing data which can be obtained and worked on at a desk.

Alan Wilson (2006) defines secondary data as:

Information that has previously been gathered for some purpose other than the current research project. The data is available either free or at a cost and can be delivered electronically by computer or in printed hard copy format.

There are two broad classifications of secondary data – internal and external. We dealt with internal data in Unit 2 on the database. In this unit we will explore external data.

The strengths and weaknesses of secondary data

Strengths

◆ It is cheap or free of charge. Costs vary but very often a full report on markets or market sectors can be put together very quickly and cheaply.

◆ It may provide an answer to the problem – this will save enormous time and effort.

◆ It can guide or provide direction for primary work.

◆ It can suggest methodologies for data collection.

◆ It can indicate problems with particular methodologies.

◆ It can provide historic or comparative data to enable longitudinal studies.

Weaknesses

◆ It is not related to the research question and the temptation may be to force the data to fit the question.

◆ It may not be directly comparable. This is particularly the case in international markets where markets may be defined differently. For example, data on the low-alcohol drinks market varies from market to market as definitions of 'low' alcohol change.

◆ Data may be incomplete. For example, the cross-channel trade in drinks and to-bacco is significant but not included in official statistics.

◆ Data may relate to certain markets – for example, data on food markets may relate to the retail trade rather than to the retail and catering markets, or vice versa. Pan-national studies will certainly find this. In many countries, a significant amount of the retail trade is through street markets. This is very hard to quantify. In this case it may be possible to weight data or use other techniques to complete the data set.

◆ It may not be available. It may be that there are certain markets that are not ad-equately covered – for example, in Europe, data on the Belgian or Dutch market is often hard to obtain as these are relatively small markets within the EU.

◆ The data may have been gathered for a particular purpose. Production statistics in certain markets are unreliable. Data may be presented to portray a company or gov-ernment in a more favourable light. We see this in the UK with the ongoing debate of how unemployment figures should be presented. Information that is reviewed without access to the methodology should be viewed with suspicion and other data sources should be brought in to confirm the data under review.

◆ Data for international markets may be more expensive and unreliable. Secondary data in certain markets may not be up to date. It may be collated at a different level. For example, your client may be interested in chocolate-coated biscuits but data only covers the total market for baked goods. A common problem is data that has been gathered at manufacturing selling price and researchers take this as the retail value of the market. You need to be quite clear at what point in the value chain data has been captured. Is it retail or ex-factory?

◆ Data for international markets may be in a foreign language. Translating costs in business markets are very expensive.

◆ Time series data may be interrupted by definition changes, for example the recent announcement by the British government about changes to the way in which infla-tion is calculated.

Evaluating secondary data

When looking at published research reports, the user should ask the following questions:

◆ Who published the study?

◆ Was it a national government?

◆ Was it a trade association?

◆ What is the nature of the organization?

◆ Is the publisher of the data the same as the organization that collected it?

◆ For what purpose was the data collected?

◆ Is the study designed to sell a service?

◆ Is it designed to counter negative publicity?

◆ Is it designed to generate publicity?

◆   When was the data gathered?

◆   Is it relevant?

◆   How was the data collected?

◆   Was the data capture mechanism reliable?

◆   Was it a self-selecting sample?

◆   Who collected the data?

◆   Are they independent?

◆   Are they trained?

◆   Are they members of a professional body?

◆   What sample was used?

◆   How reliable is the data?

◆   Is raw data presented?

◆   Can I replicate the study?

◆   Is the methodology included?

◆   Can I test the data for accuracy?

◆   Is the data comparable?

Sources of secondary data

There is a vast range of sources of secondary data, and the emergence of the Internet as a key information consolidator and provider has increased the availability of information to the desk researcher. It has increased access to previously remote information, for example data held in libraries overseas, and it has increased the ability to distribute this information. We will look later at online sources and methodology.

Data on markets and organizations can be obtained from many different sources. An able researcher will be flexible and innovative in their approach to information searches, and the most unlikely sources can reveal important information.

For example, the publications of the HR department in a certain company told a researcher about the staffing levels at particular factories in India which had been classified as confidential by the corporate affairs and marketing departments.

List of sources

One of the best aids to secondary researchers are lists of sources.

The specialists in this area are Euromonitor and Croners.

Euromonitor publishes a range of information directories. These include the following:

Companies

◆   *Global Market Share Planner:* 7 volume set

◆   *Major Market Share Companies: Americas*

◆   *Major Market Share Companies: Asia-Pacific*

- ♦ *Major Market Share Companies: Eastern Europe, Middle East and Africa*
- ♦ *Major Performance Rankings*
- ♦ *Market Share Tracker*
- ♦ *World Leading Global Brand Owners*

Countries

- ♦ *Asian Marketing Data and Statistics*
- ♦ *European Marketing Data and Statistics*
- ♦ *International Marketing Data and Statistics*
- ♦ *Latin American Marketing Data and Statistics*
- ♦ *The Enlarged European Union: A Statistical Handbook*
- ♦ *World Consumer Lifestyles on The Internet*
- ♦ *World Economic Factbook*
- ♦ *World Economic Prospects*
- ♦ *World Health Databook*
- ♦ *World Marketing Data and Statistics on the Internet*

Business information sources

- ♦ *Asia-Pacific Marketing Information Sourcebook*
- ♦ *World Retail Directory and Sourcebook*

Try looking at the Euromonitor website at www.euromonitor.com.

Other research directory services are available from www.marketresearch.com.

Other companies providing this type of service include:

- ◆ IMRI publishes a list of market research reports and agencies worldwide. Details at http://www.imriresearch.com/

- ◆ *Croners Executive Companion* and *Croners Office Companion* includes a list of business information services. These are available on- and off-line. Details are at www.croner.co.uk

- ◆ www.europa.eu./index_en.htm: A listing of information sources in the EU.

Governments

Governments publish vast quantities of data about the economy and society. Much of this data forms the basis of commercial services, provided at some cost by research firms. For example, the geo-demographic profiling services draw heavily on census data. These publications are very cheap and it is always worth checking to see what is available. Certain governments are making this data available online. The US government is exceptional and the UK's e-government initiative is slowly opening up data sources to online enquiry. A good example of this is the trade invest website which can be found at the address:

> https://www.uktradeinvest.gov.uk/

Other sources can be identified through the following sites:

> www.direct.gov.uk
>
> www.statistics.gov.uk

UK online is a general guide to government online services whilst www.statistics.gov.uk is the website of National Statistics, the statistical service of the UK government.

There is also a statistical service for the European Union and this provides comparative data across all member countries. This can be found at:

> http://epp.eurostat.ec.europa.eu

Other national governments have their own statistical services and these can normally be accessed online.

The UN statistical service offers links through to these sites at:

> http://unstats.un.org/unsd/methods/inter-natlinks/sd_natstat.htm

National and international data sources and links are available also via the Euromonitor website or by searching on Google or other search engines.

The US census also provides excellent international data at:

> http://www.census.gov/ipc/www/idb/Activity

Trade organizations

This is a broad category of information providers that include:

◆ Trade associations

◆ The trade press

◆ Professional institutes

◆ Chambers of commerce

◆ Regulatory bodies and pressure groups.

Trade associations

These exist for almost every industrial sector. Some publish amazing details on their members' activities. Associations such as the BMRA publish annual reviews of the market research industry for its members. A directory of trade associations is published by CBD and this identifies trade associations with contact details and details of activities. These can be found at www.cbdresearch.com.

Trade press

The trade press is invaluable as a source of up-to-date information on markets and companies. Almost every trade is represented, and titles like *Pig Farmer Weekly*, *Tunnels and Tunnelling*, *Wood Based Panelling International*, *The Grocer*, *Advertising Age* and *Off Licence News* give an indication of the range of sources that are available. The journalists quickly become experts in their field and they too are worth contacting. Details of trade titles can be found in the *Advertisers' Annual*.

Web address: www.hollis-publishing.com.

For international press, *Willings Press Guide* is an alternative source both on- and offline. Online they are at www.willingspress.com.

Professional institutes

These institutes generally represent individuals within the profession and some provide excellent data on their industries. The CIM is a good example. It has a wide range of information on its website and supports members through its knowledge centre and library in Cookham. Hopefully, you have already used the website. It is at www.cim.co.uk.

Chambers of commerce

These can be very helpful for organizations, particularly in overseas markets, where commitment to the Chambers' mission is sometimes greater than in the UK.

The British Chambers of Commerce website is at www.britishchambers.org.uk.

The world organization is the World Chambers Federation and their web address is at http://www.iccuk.net/.

Regulatory bodies and pressure groups

The activities of organizations like the Financial Services Authority, the Advertising Standards Authority and Oftel generate information on the sectors they cover.

Look at the Advertising Standards Authority website at www.asa.org.uk.

Pressure groups like Greenpeace or Action on Smoking and Health (ASH) can provide data on the industries they monitor and causes they represent. www.ash.org.uk. has a statistical report on smoking and smoking behaviour.

Trade unions and other member organizations can provide useful data. For example, the Salmon and Trout Association covers the market for fly fishing through its activities aimed at preserving habitat and stocks.

Financial data

Investment houses and stockbrokers produce regular reports on the activities of their target companies. The briefings that inform these reports often contain useful market and strategic data that can be extremely revealing.

The press

The *Financial Times* and *Wall Street Journal* are required reading for marketing professionals, and their services include online archives. Other national and local press can be accessed for relevant data.

The *FT* and *Wall Street Journal* are at: www.ft.com and www.wsj.com, respectively.

Specialist services

Information about companies

The best source of information in the United Kingdom is Companies House; all limited companies are obliged by law to lodge financial and other information at Companies House. The Companies House website also has a range of links to international disclosure of company data.

Companies House is found online at www.companieshouse.gov.uk.

Other organizations provide information on companies. Services such as Dunn and Bradstreet and Kompass are excellent commercial sources of company information.

Information on markets

There are hundreds of companies providing secondary or published data on markets.

A full list can be accessed at the MRS website: www.mrs.org.

Some of the more important providers include:

◆ **Nielsen** – provides data on media and advertising spend and a range of data to industry. Visit them at: www.acnielsen.co.uk

◆ **BMRB** – a leading UK research agency that provides the Target Group Index.

Insight: The Target Group Index (TGI)

This is a valuable resource to marketers and allows customer data to be enhanced in a number of ways. It also provides a useful insight into diverse markets. It is a continuous survey where data collection runs throughout the year so that seasonality does not skew results. TGI yields information on the usage of over 4000 brands in 500 product areas for those aged 15+. It is updated four times a year on a rolling quarterly basis.

The survey is based on a sample size of c.25,000 interviews per annum. Results are weighted to match known demographic profiles and re-weighted to the National Readership Survey. A self-completion questionnaire is placed with selected respondents at the end of BMRB's Access Omnibus survey.

TGI data is used to assist the understanding of target markets to aid marketing and advertising decisions. The data helps the users of TGI to optimize their marketing and advertising receipts/expenditures.

Source: www.bmrb-tgi.co.uk

Syndicated research services

Companies like Mintel, Euromonitor, and Frost and Sullivan provide what are known as syndicated or multi-client studies on a huge range of markets. These are published market research studies that are available to anybody who wishes to buy them. Prices range from a few hundred to many thousands of pounds depending on the complexity of the report and number of markets covered.

Typically, reports will cover:

◆ Market size, structure and trends

◆ Import, export and production data

◆ Key players' competitive profiles including financial data

◆ Market share data

◆ Advertising and marketing communications spend.

Details can be found at the following websites:

www.mintel.com

www.euromonitor.com

www.frost.com.

Activity 4.1

Look at some or all of these websites. They have been shown to be useful sources of research or data on the online sector.

www.clickz.com/stats	www.intersperience.com
www.forrester.com	www.oracle.com
www.ncr.com	www.gartner.com
www.broadvision.com	www.accenture.com
www.pwc.com	www.bcg.com
www.idc.com	www.bitpipe.com
www.iabuk.net	www.ovum.com

Evaluate them against the following criteria:
◆ Name of company
◆ Business sector
◆ Research company, hardware supplier, software supplier, consultancy, trade association
◆ Quality of data
◆ Range of data
◆ Credibility
◆ Accessibility
◆ Recency
◆ Geographic scope
◆ Sector coverage
◆ Cost
◆ Data collection method.

Follow the links and, if appropriate, add them to your favourites list.

Online aggregators

The development of the Internet and its diverse capabilities has lead to the emergence of a new breed of information providers who aggregate or bring together information from diverse sources and allow access on a subscription basis or for a one-off payment. Examples include general services like Hoovers, Profound and Lexis Nexis, and specialist services like the World Advertising Research Centre (WARC) or MAD which covers the UK marketing press. These may contain translations from a range of international publications.

Details can be found at the following websites:

www.mad.co.uk

www.profound.com

www.hoovers.com

www.lexisnexis.com

www.warc.com.

Information on online markets

There is a great deal of information on the Internet on online markets. Not all of it is reliable. The government, as indicated above, is often the most reliable source and there are more reputable suppliers in the market. The best sources for online research are often based in the United States, but there are a range of other useful suppliers.

Other sources include:

◆ CRM technology companies for example www.oracle.com

◆ Management consultancy www.bcg.com

◆ IT consultants www.accenture.com

Searching online

The fastest growing area of research today is that carried out online, and the area of secondary research is no different. The problem is that with such a huge array of sources available, where do we start looking.

If you know the URL or web address, then you can go online and go directly to the site. From this site a series of links may be followed and this process can yield useful information. If you do not know the URL or your search is more general, then the starting point is a search engine or directory.

Search engines

Search engines use 'spiders' or 'webbots' to go out and search the web and create a database of sites, perhaps with the assistance of human editors. This database is then matched against the search terms or keywords entered by the user in the search engine.

Some examples of search engines include:

Alta Vista	www.altavista.com
Google	www.google.com
	www.goggle.co.uk
Lycos	www.lycos.com
Northern Light	www.northernlight.com.
Yahoo	www.yahoo.com

Successful searching online

Successful online searching will be achieved if the search terms are properly defined. Careful phrasing of the search term and creative use of Boolean (logical) operators can help.

Boolean operators are usually found in the advance search section in the search engine or directory. These help the browser search the Web.

The simplest of these are the words AND, NOT and OR, or the symbols '+' (AND) and '−' (NOT). Others may allow the use of 'proximity operators', such as 'followed by' or 'near'. These can help refine search terms and produce more relevant results.

For example, 'MRS and UK not USA' would return pages containg 'MRS' and 'UK', but exclude those containing 'USA'.

Most engines may have advanced search facilities which employ Boolean operators in a more user-friendly format. The use of Google's advance search feature can reduce the number of results for any search term to far more manageable and relevant numbers.

There are lists of search engines at www.searchability.com and www.virtualfreesites.com.

Social networking sites, newsgroups, blogs and discussion forums

Newsgroups exist for almost every topic under the sun, including marketing research. Newsgroups can be useful sources of information and also for establishing opinions on products and services. Some companies monitor newsgroups for research purposes and some seed newsgroups with product information and recommendations. This is a dubious practice if it is not done transparently and if uncovered can lead to the user being barred from the service.

Most search engines allow searches for groups. Try www.groups.google.com.

Blogs can be very useful sources of information and there are significant resources available on research and marketing. Search via http://blogsearch.google.com, to find relevant content. www.technorati.com will allow you to monitor blogs and www.boardtracker.com does the same for discussion boards.

Social networking sites are useful to get a deeper understanding of how your target market is talking about your products and services. Facebook is already using volunteered profile data to target members with advertising messages.

Data fusion

Latest trends in the management of research and data have involved data fusion techniques. For example from our own customer database may be enhanced with attributed, anonymous data from research based on known characteristics, for example, post code or media viewing behaviour. This can then be linked to geo-demographic data such as ACORN and Mosaic via the post code and once the geo-demographic code is known this can link to lifestyle and behavioural data via Axcioms' Personicx system and BMRB's TGI data.

The result is a statistically valid model of consumer behaviour and this can have value in determining marketing approaches. It is always vital to get expert advice on this as the sample size for analysis can become very small.

Summary

In this unit we looked at definitions of secondary research, and looked at the strengths and limitations of research. These were:

◆ Strengths

  ◆ It is cheap or free of charge.

  ◆ It may provide an answer to the problem; this will save enormous time and effort.

  ◆ It can guide or provide direction for primary work.

  ◆ It can suggest methodologies for data collection.

  ◆ It can indicate problems with particular methodologies.

  ◆ It can provide historic or comparative data to enable longitudinal studies.

◆ Weaknesses

  ◆ It is not related to the research question and the temptation may be to force the data to fit the question.

  ◆ It may not be directly comparable.

  ◆ Data may be incomplete.

  ◆ It may not be available.

  ◆ The data may have been gathered for a particular purpose.

We looked at the range of sources that are available to the researcher, including:

◆ Government data

◆ Trade associations

◆ Professional institutes

◆ Pressure groups

◆ Regulatory bodies

◆ Financial institutions

◆ Company data

◆ Online aggregators

◆ Directories

◆ The trade press

◆ National press

◆ Specialist companies

◆ Syndicated services.

We saw that almost anything published on or by companies is capable of yielding useful data on companies, industries and markets.

We also explored secondary data relating to companies' markets and online markets. We explored how search engines and directories work and the use of Boolean operators in helping searches on the Internet.

We looked at the online market and explored ways of maximizing the effectiveness of searching online.

Finally we looked at data fusion.

Bibliography

Crouch, S. and Housden, M. (2003) *Marketing Research for Managers*, Oxford: Elsevier Butterworth-Heinemann, 3rd edition

Wilson, A. (2006) *Marketing Research: An Integrated Approach*, FT Prentice Hall, 2nd edition

Websites

National Statistics (2005) www.statistics.gov.uk

MRS (2007) www.mrs.org

Unit 5 Observation research

Learning objectives

After completing this unit you will be able to:

◆ Define observation research

◆ Understand the methods of observation research

◆ Understand and define the role of audits in marketing research

◆ Understand the application of mystery shopping techniques

◆ Identify online observation techniques

◆ Outline the ethical issues in observation research.

Table 5.1: Learning outcomes and knowledge and skills requirements

Learning outcomes	Knowledge and skills requirements
4.2 Evaluate the various procedures used for observing behaviour	Categories of observation (natural v. contrived, visible v. hidden, structured v. unstructured, mechanized v. human, participant v. non-participant)
	Audits and scanner-based research
	Television viewing measurement
	Internet monitoring
	Mystery shopping

Key definitions

Observation – A non-verbal means of obtaining primary data as an alternative or complement to questioning (MRS, 2007).

Panels – A permanent representative sample maintained by a market research agency from which information is obtained on more than one occasion either for continuous research or for ad hoc projects (MRS, 2007).

Audit – The measurement of product volume and value through the distribution network. Audit may be wholesale, retail or consumer.

> **Mystery shopping** – The collection of information from retail outlets, showrooms and so on, by people trained to observe, experience, record and measure the customer service process while posing as ordinary members of the public (MRS, 2007).
>
> **Peoplemeter** – The mechanical device used by BARB to collect data on TV audiences in the United Kingdom.
>
> **EPOS** – Electronic Point Of Sale equipment.
>
> **Cookie** – A file stored on your hard drive by a website and used to identify your computer and other information including preferences for using that site.
>
> **Ethnographic research** – Observation involving total immersion in the life of the subject.

Study guide

This unit should take you around two hours to complete.

Introduction

Observation research is one of the fastest growing areas of marketing research. Techniques such as mystery shopping and audits are growing in popularity as the need to ensure customer satisfaction is growing and the technical ability to monitor individuals' behaviour expands.

Our online behaviour can be tracked even to the extent of being able to trace the search terms used to access a particular website.

The use of CCTV and video means that the average UK consumer is caught on camera many times a day. This of course raises ethical considerations that we discussed earlier. Observation is, however, a tried and tested technique in marketing research.

Examples of commonly-used observation research:

◆ Mystery shopping to check service delivery

◆ Media consumption for example BARB TV audience measurement

◆ Advertising tests using eye-movement cameras to check the response

◆ Research in the home to explore patterns of consumption

◆ Concealed cameras in supermarket fixtures to see which products are looked at before final selection, and to assess the impact of shelf position.

Definitions of observation research

The MRS (2007) defines observation as 'A non-verbal means of obtaining primary data as an alternative or complement to questioning'.

Wilson defines (2006) it as 'a data gathering approach where information on the behaviour of people, objects and organizations is collected without any questions being asked of the participant'.

Observation strengths

◆ It is not dependent on the respondents' memory. It records exactly what has happened, not what the respondent believes has happened.

◆ The potential for bias in research is reduced as the researcher is the witness of behaviour rather than actively asking for information – the way an interviewer asks for information can influence responses.

◆ Mechanical recording of observed behaviour may reduce the incidence of reporting errors.

◆ It does not rely on the verbal skills of a respondent to describe the behaviour.

◆ It measures what has happened, not what respondents say that they will do in a certain situation.

◆ It can counter the high refusal rates in some markets.

◆ It can be used to monitor behaviour preceding an action. For example, picking up and looking at competing products before making a final decision.

◆ It does not interfere with the respondents' day-to-day life. It is their activity that is of interest. They do not have to fill in diaries or complete questionnaires.

Disadvantages of observation techniques

◆ Observation does not measure the reasons for certain behaviour. It cannot uncover motivation or attitudes.

◆ Observation cannot measure the likelihood of repeat behaviour.

◆ Only public behaviour can be assessed. Private behaviour is very difficult to research in this way although efforts have been made to manage this process.

The role of observation in revealing behaviour is most obvious when dealing with the expression of behaviour that may be viewed as antisocial or revealing a negative view of the individual. In surveys of smoking behaviour, respondents have been shown to under-report the number of cigarettes they smoke by up to 100 per cent. The same applies to alcohol units. Very often GPs will write cigarettes smoked as 10/20; 10 being the reported number, 20 the more likely figure.

Categories of observation research

Wilson (2006) identifies five different categories of observation research.

Natural	Contrived
Rather like David Attenborough and mountain gorillas, customers are observed in their natural state	The researcher sets up an observation situation
Respondents may be observed going around a supermarket, browsing a website and so on	This may be a supermarket fixture set up in a room or children playing with new toys with the researcher present
They are not aware that they are being observed	Customers are aware that they are being observed

Visible	Hidden
Customers are aware that observation is taking place because they can see the recording equipment	Respondents know that they are being observed but cannot see the observer or recording equipment
Structured	**Unstructured**
Observers keep a tally or count of certain behaviours	Observers record or make notes on all aspects of the observed behaviour
Mechanical	**Human**
The installation of equipment to measure behaviour	More appropriate for complex behaviour involving multiple interactions
Participant	**Non-participant**
The observer participates in the observed behaviour, for example, in mystery shopping	The behaviour is observed remotely

Insight: Telephone man

Observational research by Abbott Meade Vickers for British Telecommunications in-formed an advertising strategy that aimed to get men spending more time using the telephone. Observation found that men spent less time on the telephone, generally stood whilst talking on the phone and passed the phone to their partner when family or social events were being discussed.

The campaign that was developed from this involved a student ringing home, the phone was answered by her father who said 'I'll fetch your mother'. The student said 'I phoned to talk to you'. A surprised father then enjoys his chat with his daughter. The strap line 'it's good to talk' followed.

Observation methodologies

There are a range of observational techniques that are used throughout the research in-dustry. Many of these take advantage of new technology.

Audits and scanner-based observation

An audit measures product movement and consumption through the value chain. There are three types of audit – wholesale, retail and home.

The use of EPOS and hand-held scanning devices has changed this sector of the market significantly over the last 10 years.

Audits have been in place for some time, but the process of carrying them out was far more time-consuming than it is today. Researchers used to do stock counts looking at stock delivered into retail stores, stock out and stock remaining. This would give a clear idea of retail sales in the period under consideration. Companies still carry out this work in smaller stores to verify wastage and stock loss through theft, but the use of EPOS technology has significantly reduced the amount of time taken to produce results.

Companies like Nielsen and TNS are significant players in this market. Nielsen's services include Retail Measurement Services and Homescan TNS' services include TNS Superpanel.

Retail Measurement Services

Retail Measurement Services provides data on product movement, market share, distribution, price and other market-sensitive information. Using in-store scanning of product codes and store visits by professional auditors, Nielsen offers a complete portfolio of sample and census information across the food, household, health and beauty, durables, confectionery and beverage products industries.

Retail Measurement Services help to gauge:

◆ Product penetration

◆ Overall product performance

◆ Distribution intensity

◆ Promotional effectiveness

◆ Price sensitivity.

Through this service, Nielsen measures and tracks sales volume, selling price, observed promotion and merchandising execution, encompassing an organization's own brands as well as competitive brands. This can help long-term strategic planning or tactical decision-making.

Homescan

Homescan was launched in 1989 and covers 14,000 UK households and 210,000 households in 27 countries worldwide. Data is captured on costumer packaged goods including non- bar coded and fresh produce. Data is captured on a continuous basis and can be used to explore:

◆ Market dynamics

◆ Promotional output

◆ Brand switching

◆ Loyalty

◆ Parallel consumption

◆ Repeat purchase

◆ Customer demographics and lifestyle

Source: www.Nielsen.com/products/cps_homescan_detail.shtml

TNS Superpanel

Superpanel is a consumer panel and provides purchasing information on all main grocery markets. It was launched in 1991 and consists of 15,000 households, demographically and regionally balanced to offer a representative picture of the GB marketplace.

Data is collected twice weekly via electronic terminals in the home, with purchases being recorded via home-scanning technology. All household members are asked to record details of purchases they make and bring into the home. This is done by using a palm computer equipped with a laser scanner to scan the barcodes on products they buy plus some details from a codebook.

Panel members enter information on products bought through a sequence of questions asked by the kit.

◆ 'Purchaser identity' (scanned from codebook).

◆ 'Shop name' (scanned from codebook).

◆ 'Total amount spent' (entered manually from till roll receipt).

◆ 'Product' (barcode scanned).

Details for non-barcoded fresh food products are collected by answering specific on-screen questions displayed on the palm kit.

The terminal is also programmed to recognize random weight barcodes which appear on packs that come in a range of different weights. These are common among markets such as cheese and meat. In these cases the weight of the item is collected on-screen.

Panel members are also asked to return their till receipts. These are scanned and put through an optical character recognition process which extracts the price paid for each item bought. This price information is then linked back to the details of the same shopping trip scanned in by that panel member. In this way, the workload on panel members is reduced to a minimum, and their recruitment and retention made easier.

The terminal software automatically records the date and time when each shopping trip is recorded, and which barcodes were keyed in rather than scanned due to poor print quality on difficult pack designs. This information is used for quality control purposes.

When not being used for scanning the kit is normally kept in a modem, directly linked to the power supply and a telephone socket. This allows data capture (or polling) to take place overnight twice weekly without disturbing panel members.

Source: www.superpanel.TNSglobal.com/superpanel.

Home audits

In the past, home audit methodology has included the keeping of written records. Respondents would keep a diary of behaviour. These are still used in markets or by companies where scanning technology is not available, and to measure behaviour that is not capable of being scanned, for example meal times and number of people eating together. Home audits can also involve waste bin audits. Though not a pleasant task, this allows researchers to evaluate product consumption or usage rate in the home.

The use of observation equipment in stores can produce data on other areas of shoppers' behaviour, e.g. the route around the store, or the way that they browse a retail fixture.

Audit data can produce a huge range of analysis, and the services of Nielsen and TNS provide the raw material for the marketing management of the retail and grocery marketing sector.

This data includes:

◆ Market share

◆ Brand share

◆ Brand loyalty

◆ Category loyalty

◆ Retail sector analysis

◆ Retail share

◆ Retail price checks

◆ Average basket

◆ Sales promotion responses and so on.

The services are available internationally and most European markets are covered.

Some European markets remain harder to audit through traditional means, and statistical weightings are used to produce a full picture of retail sales. Other markets can be audited but the use of scanning technology may mean that more low-tech solutions are needed to carry out the task. For example, in Indonesia, sales of cigarettes are made from kiosks that may sell 1–2 cigarettes from a pack at a time. This is hard to measure!

Media measurement

The measurement of media is a key element of observation research. The most important of these in the United Kingdom is the Broadcaster's Audience Research Board (BARB). It provides the measurement service for television viewing in the United Kingdom. In early 2003, the contract for TV-viewing measurement was changed. This new contract is due to run for 5–8 years. The old panel which was set up in 1991 was replaced with a new panel recruited from scratch over the last two years. The main change is to increase the size of the panel from 4300 homes to 5100 homes and covers 11,500 viewers.

This reflects the changes in the media landscape in the United Kingdom. In 1983 there were only three TV channels in the United Kingdom; today there are hundreds. The old sample was not large enough to ensure robust data on smaller TV audiences.

Other changes to the panel design were reported by BARB to include:

◆ Removal of demographic disproportionality.

◆ The undersampling of downmarket audiences has ended and the entire panel is now proportionate to the population.

◆ Improved geographic representation.

◆ Regional panels will be more representative of their proportion of the UK population. London, for example, has 20 per cent of the UK population, but under the old BARB system had only 12 per cent of panel homes. Under the new system it will have 17 per cent of panel homes.

◆ Revised panel controls (the aspects against which the panel is recruited to ensure it is representative – such as age, social class and so on).

◆ Multi-channel television homes will be recruited with a greater level of panel controls than on the previous system.

◆ A more detailed weighting scheme to introduce a greater level of representativeness to the reporting sample.

♦ An increased annual Establishment Survey (the source of population estimates and penetration figures on which panel controls are based) of 50,000 interviews to provide more robust estimates, particularly by platform.

♦ Updated metering equipment that is non-intrusive, upgradeable and therefore future-proofed.

Source: BARB 2007.

Case study: BARB – watching you watching them

The television measurement service provides television audience data on a minute-by-minute basis for channels received within the United Kingdom. The data is available for reporting nationally as well as at the regional level.

Viewing estimates are obtained from panels of television-owning households representing the viewing behaviour of the 24+ million households within the United Kingdom. The panels are selected to be representative of each ITV and BBC region. Panel homes are selected via a multi-stage stratified and unclustered sample design. This ensures that the panel is fully representative of households across the whole of the United Kingdom. Each panel is maintained against a range of individual and household characteristics (panel controls). As the estimates for the large majority of the panel controls are not available from census data, it is necessary to conduct surveys (Establishment Survey) to obtain this information.

The Establishment Survey is a random probability survey carried out on a continuous basis involving some 50,000 interviews per year. The nature of this survey ensures that any changes within the characteristics of the population can be identified. Panel controls can therefore be updated and panel household representation, adjusted to ensure representativeness, is maintained. In addition to being the prime source of television population information, the Establishment Survey also generates a pool of potential recruits from which panel member homes are recruited. Each of the panel member households have all their television receiving equipment (sets, video cassette recorders, set-top box decoders, etc.) electronically monitored by a 'peoplemeter' monitoring system. This system automatically identifies and records the channel to which each television set is tuned when switched on and all viewing involving a VCR (recording, playback, viewing through the VCR, etc.). In addition, the metering system incorporates the capability to 'fingerprint' videotapes during recording sessions and to subsequently identify such recorded material when played back (time-shifted viewing).

All permanent household residents and guests declare their presence in a room whilst a television set is on by pressing an allocated button on a handset. The metering system monitors all registrations made by each individual.

Throughout each day, the meter system stores all the viewing undertaken by the entire household. Each night the panel household is contacted by the processing centre by telephone to collect the stored data. This procedure is carried out on every home each day to produce 'overnight' television viewing data.

Source: www.barb.co.uk

Other media are audited in different ways – some are based on observation, some on other research methods.

The leading company for Internet audience research is Nielsen with its Net ratings service. They cover a range of online measurements including site traffic, video streaming and social networking sites, browsing behaviour and through buzz metrics the role of viral and word of mouth. The service can be reviewed at www.nielsen-netratings.com. Other companies operating in this market include comScore.

In the UK the launch of of JICIMS, the Joint Industry Committee for Internet Measurement Systems marks the coming of age of the online media market. JICIMS can be found at www.jicims.org.uk

In the UK, the measurement of poster sites is carried out though observation. Video cameras are used to measure the number of full faces looking at a poster. This data is used to help the media sales people.

A really useful site that discusses the full range of media research services is Zenith Optimedia Marketer's Portal, at www.marketersportal.com/. The A to Z listing covers the full range of research services for media.

Activity 5.1

Go to www.marketersportal.com and and review the information sources that are available. See what you can find out about:

◆　　Postar, the poster research organization in the UK

◆　　Nielsen Net Ratings

◆　　NRS, the National readership survey

◆　　ABC, the Audit Bureau of Circulation which provides an independent verification of a claimed circulation figure for newspapers.

Other observation techniques

Ethnography

Ethnography is a research technique that has been used in the social sciences for some time and is increasingly used in marketing. Ethnographic research involves total immersion in the life of the subject and researchers may spend a considerable amount of time with the subject of the research.

Results may be recorded on camera or written down post-experience. The research may for example look at family interaction with a product or brand and may reveal depth of insight to inform market positioning.

Ethnographic research has been used by researchers looking at the problem of football hooliganism in the United Kingdom. Researchers travel with known hooligans and later record their experiences. As you might imagine, would be impossible to use other techniques to research this behaviour.

Mechanical observation

A range of mechanical observation techniques are used in observation research which include:

Psychogalvanometers

This measures the respondents' reaction to a message. It uses the same techniques as a lie detector, measuring the electrical resistance of the skin. The amount of sweat on the skin increases during arousal and it is this that is measured. It is most often used for pre-testing advertising and copy.

Pupilmeters

Pupilmeters measure the same responses through a measurement of pupil dilation.

Eye cameras

Eye cameras are used to track the movement of the eye around an object, maybe a piece of creative or a retail fixture. This method has been used on websites' research to explore the navigation of sites and may be combined with a mechanical record of key strokes or mouse movement.

Tachistoscopes

Reveal the test material in microsecond bursts. The respondents' ability to recall detail is measured. Amongst other uses, it is believed to predict advertising effectiveness.

Mystery shopping

Mystery shopping is defined by the MRS (2007) as 'The collection of information from retail outlets, showrooms and so on by people trained to observe, experience, record and measure the customer service process posing as ordinary members of the public.'

This may be done by companies assessing the activities of competitors in the market or by companies assessing the performance of their own sales staff.

Wilson (2006) identifies three main purposes for mystery shopping:

◆ To act as a diagnostic tool identifying failings and weak points in service delivery

◆ To encourage and reward staff by linking outcomes to appraisal and reward and incentive schemes

◆ To assess competitors by benchmarking service and other standards.

Mystery shopping can help the process of managing the customer experience, provide a baseline from which to measure improvement in service and related areas. Ultimately through enhanced customer experience it should produce real value for the brand.

Mystery shoppers should present facts rather than opinions and these may include the shopping environment as well as interactions between the researcher and staff. This is designed to reduce researcher bias.

A checklist for the management of mystery shopping:

◆ There must be careful recruitment of mystery shoppers as staff may become familiar with them; they need to be replaced and or rotated across products and services.

- Age, gender and appearance of shoppers may affect the experience and the shopper needs to fall within the target market.

- The shopper must be natural and to make the experience as close to life as possible.

- Training and supervision is very important.

- Data capture and recording needs to be carefully considered. Some mystery shopping for example has involved the use of hidden cameras.

- Analysis of the data can be highly subjective and a formal structure for analysis might be needed to ensure the valid comparison of results between retail outlets – the use of some form of recording equipment may help this task.

Activity 5.2

Review the MRS guidelines on mystery shopping at www.mrs.org.uk

Insight: This dealer bites

Mystery shopping is used extensively in the car market. The brand advertising of the leading car companies is ultimately reinforced or compromised by the sales people staffing the showroom. One mystery shopper described the experience of entering the sales showroom as like 'being thrown into a shark-filled pool'.

One of the world's largest providers of mystery shopping is GAPbuster and they can be found at www.gapbuster.com.

Online observation

We have already mentioned the use of observation techniques in designing websites. However, the characteristics of the Internet allow for a lot of data to be captured through remote observation. The use of cookies allows the website owner to identify repeat visits.

A cookie is a text file placed on the browser's computer that allows it to be identified on subsequent visits. A cookie may contain the computer's address or details of a customer registration. This means that when the customer logs on, a personalized greeting can be made or passwords provided. Cookies cannot extract information.

Most online retailers use this system; for example, Amazon will drive content to particular customers based on their previous behaviour. Browser behaviour through the site can also be captured and used. This has been used to tailor-make print brochures based on customers' browsing behaviour through the site. We can track where browsers have come from and where they go to after leaving the site.

Ethics in observation research

There are clearly significant ethical considerations in the use of observation research. The basic rule is that if observation is to take place in a situation in which behaviour could not usually be observed, then permission should be asked.

The MRS code of conduct has specific sections on mystery shopping. This includes the liaison with employees who are the subject of mystery shopping communicating the fact that the technique being used covers the organization from any data protection issue and may be motivating in itself.

How is observation research used?

Applications for observation research

There are a range of core applications for observation research. These may include:

◆ To improve customer service

◆ To improve store layout

◆ To improve staffing levels to reduce waiting time at call centres or at service points

◆ To generate information to inform reward and recognition schemes

◆ To monitor time spent on any activity, for example TV consumption

◆ To measure the amount of product consumed

◆ To look at product combinations

◆ To explore alternative product uses

◆ To explore product interaction.

International issues

The use of observation is appropriate in all markets. Indeed, in some international markets it may be the preferred method.

In addition to the usual international caveats of cost, comparability and availability of resources, for example CCTV, we have to add the problem of interpretation. The interpretation of body language, signs (semiotics) and non-verbal behaviour is culturally determined. For example, in certain African countries it is not unusual for men to hold hands as they are walking together.

In other markets, colours may mean something very different from the UK. In China, red means good luck while in other countries it means danger. In some other markets, green is the colour for danger. In the UK, white is the colour representing purity and is worn by brides at their weddings. In Japan, white is the colour of mourning, and in Brazil, purple is the colour of mourning.

International marketing is fraught with these difficulties but they are certainly not insurmountable. One way to manage this is to use James Lee's idea of self-reference criteria (Lewis and Housden, 1999). The researcher should interpret the behaviour in response to his or her own domestic culture, identify the factors affected by their cultural bias, isolate them and interpret the observation through an understanding of this bias.

Otherwise, it is important to use local agencies who can interpret the behaviour observed from their own cultural perspective. One person's aggressive argument might be a lively discussion between friends in other markets.

Summary

In this unit we looked at observation research. We looked at the types of research:

◆ Natural versus contrived

◆ Visible versus hidden

◆ Structured versus unstructured

◆ Mechanized versus human

◆ Participant versus non-participant.

In particular, we looked at the audit process, and the key suppliers of audit data in the UK – Nielsen and TNS.

We looked in depth at the role of mystery shopping in observation research and at the ethical constraints on its use. We saw that its main functions are to:

◆ Act as a diagnostic tool identifying failings and weak points in service delivery

◆ Encourage and reward staff

◆ Assess competitors.

We saw that other purposes of observational research were to:

◆ Improve customer service

◆ Improve store layout

◆ Improve staffing levels to reduce waiting time at call centres or at service points

◆ Generate information to inform reward and recognition schemes

◆ Monitor time spent on any activity, for example TV consumption

◆ Measure the amount of product consumed

◆ Look at product combinations

◆ Explore alternative product uses

◆ Explore product interaction.

International observation research was covered, and the use of self-reference criteria in the interpretation of results was advised.

We looked at the mechanical devices used for capturing data both on- and off-line.

A range of mechanical observation techniques are used in observation research. These include:

◆ Psychogalvanometers

◆ Eye cameras

◆ Tachistoscopes.

Finally, we looked at issues to do with online observation including the use of cookies.

Bibliography

Lewis, K. and Housden, M. (1999) *International Marketing*, London: Kogan Page

Wilson, A. (2006) *Marketing Research: An Integrated Approach*, FT Prentice Hall, 2nd edition

Website

BARB (2007) www.barb.co.uk

MRS (2007) www.mrs.org.uk

Unit 6 Qualitative research

Table 6.1: Learning outcomes and knowledge and skills requirements

Learning outcomes	Knowledge and skills requirements
4.3 Identify and evaluate the various techniques for collecting qualitative data	Types of research most suited to qualitative research
	Discussion guide format
	Selecting respondents
	Individual depth interviews
	Group discussions (including guidelines on group moderation, stimulus material and projective techniques)
	Using the Internet for qualitative research (online group discussions, chat rooms, blogs)
	Overview of approach to the analysis of qualitative research

Projective techniques – A form of disguised questioning that encourages participants to attribute their feelings, beliefs or motivations to another person, object or situation. Examples of projective techniques are word association, sentence completion and thematic apperception tests (ESOMAR, 2007).

Focus groups – A number of respondents gathered together to generate ideas through the discussion of, and reaction to, specific stimuli. Under the steerage of a moderator, focus groups are often used in exploratory work or when the subject matter involves social activities, habits and status (MRS, 2007).

Moderator – An individual who facilitates but does not influence a group discussion.

One-way window – A device used to allow researchers to view respondents without themselves being seen.

Depth interviews – A variety of data collection techniques, mainly for qualitative research undertaken with individual respondents rather than groups (MRS, 2007).

Topic or discussion guide – An outline of the structure, themes and timing of a focus group or depth interview.

Content analysis software – Computer software that helps with the textual analysis of qualitative research.

Respondents – An individual or organization from whom information is sought, directly or indirectly, which could, in whole or in part, form the results of a research project (MRS, 2007).

Brand personality tests – Asks respondents to describe a brand as a person.

Study guide

This unit should take you around two hours to complete. You should set aside another two hours to complete the activities outlined throughout the unit.

Introduction

Qualitative research accounts for between 10 and 15 per cent of total research expenditure in the United Kingdom. It is growing in importance as marketing professionals recognize its vital role in providing depth of understanding about customers and their behaviour. This unit will introduce you to the methods used in qualitative research and the major applications supported by this methodology.

Qualitative research defined

So how can qualitative research be defined? The MRS (2007) defines qualitative research as 'A body of research techniques which seeks insights through loosely structured, mainly verbal data rather than measurements. Analysis is interpretative, subjective, impressionistic and diagnostic'.

Crouch and Housden's (2003) definition is 'Qualitative research is so called because its emphasis lies in producing data which is rich in insight, understanding, explanation and depth of information, but which cannot be justified statistically'.

Alan Wilson (2006) in the course text defines qualitative research as 'Research that is undertaken using an unstructured research approach with a small number of carefully selected individuals to produced non quantifiable insights into behaviour motivations and attitudes'.

What are the essential characteristics of qualitative research?

◆ It is unquantifiable and is not representative of larger populations.

◆ Data collection techniques are unstructured.

◆ It involves small samples of individuals or groups of people.

◆ It seeks to reveal opinions, motivations and attitudes.

◆ It is about insight and depth of understanding.

◆ It is subject to a high degree of interpretation by skilled researchers.

◆ It often precedes quantitative work but can be independent of it.

◆ It can inform the nature of quantitative research.

Table 6.2: Key differences between qualitative and quantitative research

Comparative elements	Qualitative research	Quantitative research
Type of questions	Probing	Non-probing
Sample size	Small	Large
Information per respondent	Much	Varies
Management	Special skills	Fewer skills
Type of analysis	Subjective	Statistical
Ease of replication	Difficult	Easy
Type of research	Exploratory	Descriptive or causal
Research training needed	Psychology Sociology Consumer behaviour Marketing	Statistics Decision models Computer programming Marketing
Hardware needed	DVD recorders Digital voice recorders Web cams	Computers PDA CATI systems

Source: Adapted from AMR (2003)

Research applications

Typically qualitative work is carried out to explore what people need, care about or feel about a certain subject. It can be used for a variety of research objectives including:

◆ Exploratory research to help define problem area and develop research objectives

◆ To uncover the context of decision making

◆ To reveal brand perceptions for our brands and competitors' brands

◆ To explore the reason why people behave in the way they do; to look a the underlying motivations and attitudes behind behaviour

◆ Exploring attitudes to elements of the marketing mix, for example, advertising creative or new product testing, product development and line extensions or pack designs

◆ Creative concept testing

◆ Motivational research to define areas for quantitative research

◆ Segmentation studies

◆ Positioning studies

◆ Brand and name development.

Data collection techniques in qualitative research

Focus groups or group discussions

Wilson (2006) defines group discussions as 'depth interviews with a group of people; they differ in that they involve interaction between respondents'.

The MRS (2007) defines group discussions or focus groups as 'A number of respondents gathered together to generate ideas through the discussion of, and reaction to, specific stimuli. Under the steerage of a moderator, focus groups are often used in exploratory work or when the subject matter involves social activities, habits and status'.

Focus groups are generally made up of around 6–12 respondents. The most common number is 8. A lower number may be used when a particularly specialist topic is being discussed. The higher number would be used for a wide-ranging discussion. This design aspect is determined by the need to reflect the range of views held on a subject by the target market or concerned population.

They are run by an interviewer, usually called a moderator. This may be the same researcher who produced the research proposal, or a specialist consultant or employed from a fieldwork agency. The moderator will control the group, keeping the discussion on track and probing for further information when needed. The moderator will introduce other tasks that may occur within the group.

The main aim of the group is to ensure that the group members discuss the topic amongst themselves; the moderator's touch should be as light as possible. However, the skilled moderator will use a range of techniques to control the input of particularly vociferous members and to encourage quieter members of the group to make their contribution.

Groups will normally last between 1 to 2 hours. Discussions are generally recorded and filmed.

Groups usually occur at the beginning of a research project as they can provide very useful information to explore through other methods. Although groups may comprise the entire project.

The groups may be observed remotely and agencies offer clients the chance to view groups set up in special rooms, where the client can observe the group through a one-way window. Alternatively the group can be viewed remotely using web streaming.

The moderator can be linked by a concealed or a discrete microphone to the observers so that a particularly interesting line of discussion can be probed further.

Insight: What makes a moderator?

Sally is an open and friendly woman aged 40. She is a freelance qualitative researcher and has moved into this career after a successful period in advertising planning, where she worked at a senior level on a range of accounts. She has a degree in Psychology and holds both the CIM and MRS diplomas. She is from London but it is hard to discern any accent. She dresses conservatively. She is a good listener but can be assertive when required. These features help to make her a good moderator.

Moderators should be:

◆ Highly qualified and experienced in research and, possibly, psychology.

◆ Business-and-marketing aware. They need to be able to translate respondents' feelings into business advantage for their clients.

◆ Strong communicators, able to relate to a range of people.

◆ Hard to place regionally in terms of socio-economic class.

◆ Socially able, relaxed and friendly, but strong enough to control a room of animated, or conversely, disinterested respondents.

◆ Flexible and quick thinking, with the ability to respond to the unexpected.

Focus group discussion guide

◆ Intros – ensure everyone understands nature of the focus group and the objectives and so on, as well as that it is an independent study ... allow everyone to introduce each other! [5 mins]. As part of this – who do you work for – franchise or brand owner?

◆ What brands would you consider to be successful brands? [5 mins]

◆ Why do you think these brands are so successful? [5 mins]

◆ What is your perception of our brand [for this you will create some visual ideas]? We will base this on the following:

  ◆ If the brand was a famous personality, would it be a popstar or politician? [10 mins]

* If it were a place, where would it be? What would the weather be like? [10 mins]

Brand mapping exercise. In two groups, plot our brand on the chart against key competitors, discuss and justify.

◆ What do you feel our customers see as important? [10 mins]

◆ How do you think you can make a difference to what is important? [7.5 mins]

◆ If you were the boss, what would you do to change the image/brand, if anything? [7.5 mins]

◆ Close.

◆ Thanks, next steps and payment of incentives. [10 mins]

Stimulus material

Stimulus material may include a range of physical objects which respondents can use to reflect upon or use to express their views non-verbally. These may include:

◆ Creative samples: proofs, animated outlines of TV commercials, concept or storyboards, mail copy or print advertisements

◆ Mocked-up product packs

◆ Product samples

◆ Materials for projective work.

Recruitment of respondents

The recruitment of respondents is an important part of the process. Participants may be recruited in a number of ways:

◆ Through screening interviews at home or in the street

◆ Through professional recruitment services identified in the *Research Buyer's Guide*, or the MRS website.

The use of recruiters may save time and money but can have the drawback of recruiting 'professional' group respondents who are not typical of an audience.

Screening questions should ensure that respondents fit the overall profile of the population under consideration.

For example:

* Male

* Over 50

* Who has a home computer

* Who has bought via the Internet in the last month

* Who has no connection with the computer or research industry.

Generally, respondents' attendance is encouraged by incentives like cash payments or gifts, nd refreshments are provided. It is advisable to invite more respondents to attend than the minimum required to complete the group, as non-attendance can be an issue.

Typically, two groups per segment of interest would be carried out but more may be required if looking at sub-sectors or regional variations.

Group interviews cost between £1500 and £4500 each depending on the type of group (e.g. professional groups are more expensive), complexity and the moderator. The cost would cover all aspects of the group from recruitment, the creation of the discussion guide, running the group analysis and reporting. Group moderation is a highly skilled job, and good moderators are usually highly trained and commercially astute.

The topic or discussion guide

Creating the discussion guide

It is important to realize that a discussion guide is NOT a questionnaire. It is designed almost as an aide memoire to guide the moderator through the relatively lengthy and complex task of moderating a group of animated people.

The guide may contain outline timings and broad areas for questioning, or it may be more specific depending on the nature of the task.

The key point is that moderators should not be referring constantly to the discussion guide as this will disrupt the dynamics of the group. Positive body language and the use of eye contact are essential to the positive control of the group.

Moderators should be totally familiar with the guide before the group takes place; it should be used as a backstop to ensure that all areas have been covered and probed adequately.

The structure of a discussion guide will simply follow introduction, main body and summary but within the main body there may well be staging posts and breakout activity that need careful management.

Wilson suggests that the guide breaks the group into three distinct phases:

1   Introduction
   (a) Objectives
   (b) Personal introductions
   (c) Agenda.
2   Discussive phase
   (a) Topic areas
   (b) Stimulus material.
3   Summarizing phase
   (a) Summarizing discussion
   (b) Closing
   (c) Administration.

To summarize: The discussion guide is a route map for the group interview. It outlines a timetable of activity and highlights key stages in the process. It is not a list of questions. It covers key themes that should be covered within the group discussion and allows the moderator to mentally or physically cross off areas that have been covered.

Activity 6.1

Using Wilson's template, write a discussion guide for a car dealership client who has asked you to research new customers' experience of the sales experience. Remember to try to focus on themes rather than questions. Produce an outline timetable for a group lasting one and a half hours.

Customer focus group discussion guide

Below is an outline discussion guide suitable for a car dealership sales experience. Each of the sections could have more detail but the framework is correct. A skilled researcher could use this to carry out discussion in the group.

1 Introduction, 10 mins

(a) Objectives

(b) Rules of the road for focus group research, MRS confidentiality, consent, permission

(c) Introductions: Introduce the person next to you.

2 Discussion phase

(a) Customer service generally, 10 mins

- Experiences of really good service – why?

- Experience of a really bad service – why?

(b) The dealership, 10 mins

- What was the experience like in the dealership pre-purchase?

(c) During the negotiation, 10 mins

(d) After sales, 10 mins

(e) People, 10 mins

(f) Facilities, 10 mins

(g) Marketing Collateral, 10 mins

3 Exercise: 2 Groups projective technique: Dealership CV, 15 mins

(a) Report back and discuss

(b) Close and summary, 10 mins

(c) Other issues

(d) Key elements

(e) Thank you and gift, 5 mins

Focus groups have a number of advantages

◆　They replicate the dynamic social interactions that occur in the marketplace and may allow reluctant responders to contribute effectively.

◆　They provide rich and detailed knowledge of a subject; they are excellent for uncovering hidden motivations and in generating new ideas and insight.

◆　They are more efficient in terms of time. One focus group can be done in a day while 14 depth interviews might take at least two weeks to complete.

◆　They also allow for a range of opinions to be elicited in one group.

◆　They are cheaper per interviewee than depth interviews.

◆　They can be viewed remotely in real time and recorded for later analysis.

◆　Remote viewers can communicate additional questions or discussion points to moderators via a radio-linked earpiece.

◆　They allow interaction with physical stimuli, for example products.

◆　They can involve multiple techniques within the framework of the focus group.

Disadvantages include the following:

◆　They can be hard to control

◆　They take skill and time to analyse

◆　They can intimidate reluctant responders although the skill of the moderator is to bring out these people

◆　They can be derailed by vociferous respondents. Again the moderator should manage this.

Depth interviews

The MRS (2007) defines 'depth interviews' as a term used to 'describe a variety of data collection techniques, but mainly for qualitative research undertaken with individual respondents rather than groups'.

Usually in a study that involves depth interviews, 10–15 interviews will be carried out depending on the nature of the sample. They cost between £400 and £700 per interview.

Depth interviews have several advantages:

◆　They are conducted face to face, and body language can be interpreted.

◆　Proximity may encourage respondents to reveal more than they might in a remote interview.

◆　The respondent is the centre of attention and can be probed at length to explore issues that the researcher feels are important. This is the 'annoying child' syndrome with the researcher asking 'why' (but more subtly) until the issue is explored adequately.

◆　Group dynamics may prevent individuals expressing themselves particularly over areas that are sensitive, like income.

◆ Recruitment tends to be easier.

◆ The logistics are easier, no special rooms are needed.

◆ They reveal depth of understanding.

◆ They are flexible. The line of questioning may evolve within the interview and between interviews.

◆ They can involve a range of techniques.

Depth interviews can last up to two hours but more typically they will last around 45 minutes. They are tape recorded or videoed to enable the researcher to concentrate on the discussion and its implications rather than writing down notes.

As for group discussion, the researcher does not have a list of questions but rather a topic guide as a route map through the interview.

The location of the interview may be in the office or in the home. The main thing is that the respondent feels comfortable and relaxed.

Interviews generally take place with an individual but may involve more than one respondent if the research question is dealing with a subject in which the respondents may affect each other's decision, for example high involvement purchases like pensions or cars.

Example of depth interview discussion guide

Questions/discussion guide for in-depth interviews at the strategic level.

1 Introduction

2 Objective, permission, confidentiality

3 This research is focused on looking at how relationships can add value. The subject of the research is: Does employee behaviour at the retailer level have an impact on brand values?

4 Objectives of the interview – I am looking to understand your thoughts, opinions and feelings at a strategic level to gauge your perception of the brand and the impact of people's behaviour upon its value.

5 Discussion phase

◆ Factors considered important in the creation of a successful brand

◆ Perception of the brand

◆ What is important to customers?

◆ Staff's brand perception

◆ Retailer impacts on brand value

◆ Retail staff and positive brand image

◆ Your vision for the future for the brand

6 Close

7 Thanks and next steps

The interviewer needs to have the same or similar skills as the group moderator. The respondent must feel at ease, and techniques such as positive reinforcement and mirroring of body posture can be used. The interviewer must be skilled in managing depth interviews, and in B2B interviewing the interviewer may need a considerable amount of industry knowledge in order to ask the right questions and know when and how to probe for more information.

What are we like?

Depth interviews are used a great deal to uncover perceptions held by key audiences in a market. This may be used to establish organizational values and mission. It ensures that the current perception of an organization is known. In recent studies, depth interviews were carried out with the following type of people:

- Key suppliers
- A range of competitors
- Journalists in the national and trade press
- Trade association representatives
- Key account customers
- Trade unions
- Employee representative groups.

What do they like?

Group interviews were used by a Japanese entrant into the UK food market. The research objectives were broad and this research was part of an exploratory phase that looked at market potential for their range of instant meals. Researchers were asked to explore various potential brand names and to taste-test the existing Japanese product range. The research provided the basis for a successful European launch.

Projective techniques

Projective techniques are designed to allow respondents to 'attribute their feelings, beliefs or motivations to another person, object or situation' (ESOMAR, 2008). They are usually very interesting to administer and reveal some fascinating insight into the research problem. They have several advantages:

- They free respondents from the bonds of language and allow them to express feelings they may find hard to describe in words.

- They are engaging for respondents, are usually fun to do and get respondents motivated.

- They provide richer insight than conventional questioning: in the right hands the analysis can be extremely revealing.

- They can create excellent ideas for further exploration.

The disadvantage is that data from these techniques may be hard to interpret.

Sentence completion

This technique involves (as the term describes) simply asking respondents to complete sentences or fill in a missing word or words from a sentence. For example:

'I think that McDonald's food is . . . . '

'People who buy Dell computers are . . . .'

'CIM workbooks are . . . . '

Story completion

A set of events is related to a respondent who is asked to complete the story or say what he would have done in a similar situation. The respondent may also be asked to explain the behaviour described, for example receiving poor service in a car retailer.

Word association

This technique has been used in psychoanalysis for many years. It simply asks respondents to state the first word that comes into their head after a cue word is given. Reponses may be spoken or written down. Researchers may chain responses together to go deeper into the association or probe the reason for the association. For example, 'Skoda' and 'cheap' reveals something about the Skoda brand but respondents may be thinking about value for money and this would need to be probed further.

Cartoon completion

This involves showing the respondent a cartoon drawing. These may be single images or paired images in which one individual is talking to another. In single images, speech bubbles are left blank, or in paired drawings the second speech bubble is left blank for the respondent to complete.

Mood boards

Mood boards are collages of images that are cut from magazines and assembled, either glued or pinned on a board. This technique can reveal the associations with other products' images and colours that may not come out in conventional research. The same objective lies behind asking respondents to model images relating to a brand in plasticine or clay or to draw them on paper.

Brand personality or brand CVs

Brand personality asks respondents to describe a brand as a person. Another term is the 'brand CV' in which respondents write a mock curriculum vitae for the brand under consideration. This can be very useful in determining the accuracy of positioning in the market.

Activity 6.2

Try the brand CV task with brands of your choice. Try it with friends or colleagues. Are there any differences? Try it with Volvo and see what results you get..

Associations can also be made with objects or known people or celebrities; the reason for the association is the most important thing here. So if a car brand is described as 'Roger Moore' the researcher needs to probe to uncover the meaning of the association. Unfortunately for the brand and Roger Moore, the association in this piece of work was due to the fact that 'he was once glamorous but now past it'.

Brand mapping

It is an extension of the brand personality test that involves multiple brands. Respondents are asked to identify key attributes or dimensions of a product sector and then position brands against those relative to the competition.

This can be useful in identifying positioning and segmentation criteria and is very useful in identifying gaps in the marketplace.

The Alcopops sector was developed from this type of work. Consumers identify the fact that as children they drink fizzy, sweet, non-alcoholic drinks and as adults they drink flat, bitter or dry, alcoholic drinks. Alcopops filled the gap for sweet fizzy alcoholic drinks.

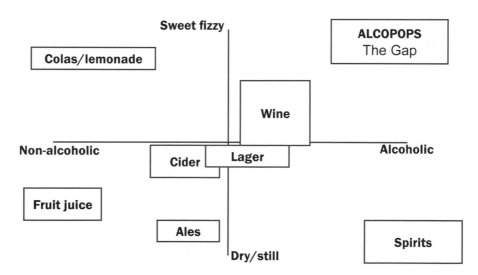

Figure 6.1: Category mapping in the drinks market

These are also known as perceptual maps and in the right hands can be very revealing. Many people, however, simply choose to use standard dimensions to build the maps, most often price and quality.

In the past, this was adequate to differentiate products in markets. Jacob's Creek, for example, entered the UK wine market as a reasonably priced, reasonably good wine. This was a sustainable position in an undifferentiated market, in which wine choices were often Blue or Black (Blue Nun or Black Tower) and luxury was a bottle of Mateus Rose.

Today, wines labelled 'Tastes Great with Chicken' and 'Tastes Great with Beef' are available. New differentiated positions in this market are hard to imagine. Maybe 'Tastes Great with Chicken Wings'!!

In most of today's competitive markets, price and quality are inadequate dimensions to make a difference or to differentiate one product from another. The dimensions can usefully be developed from research or the perceptual maps can be used to assess alternative positions in the market. For example, Lucozade was effectively repositioned as an adult fitness drink through understanding that the brand's values of aiding recovery from illness could be translated into a more positive and contemporary positioning: enabling recovery from exercise and allowing you to exercise longer.

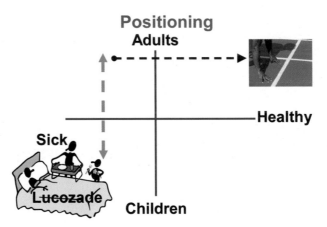

Figure 6.2: Lucozade brand repositioning

Thematic apperception tests or TAT tests

Images are shown to the respondents and they are asked to place the image in a story context. Or respondents are asked to describe what is happening and what will happen next – for example an executive boarding a business calls flight at Heathrow.

Photo sorts

Images of different people are presented and classified as to the brands they would and would not use.

Role play

Respondents are asked to act out a scene. If used in groups, it is important that the group is well-motivated and prepared to participate fully.

Role play is a pain

In a well-known example, respondents were asked to play the victim of a headache, the pain and the pain relief. Some described the pain as sharp, aggressive and violent; others described it as dull, nagging and annoying. The pain relief was either aggressive or gentle. This research led to the development of a positioning for over-the-counter pain relief.

Online qualitative research

The Web is increasingly being used for a range of research activities and this applies equally to qualitative research. This includes depth interviews and focus groups. Focus groups use chat room technology to manage the interaction. People interact through their computers.

Newsgroup technology is also used. Online notice boards are used to post messages and a group of people exchange information about a specific topic (Figure 6.3).

Respondents are often recruited by e-mail and agree to participate at a certain time, at a certain URL. Each member is able to read the responses of other members and respond to their comments as if in a group situation.

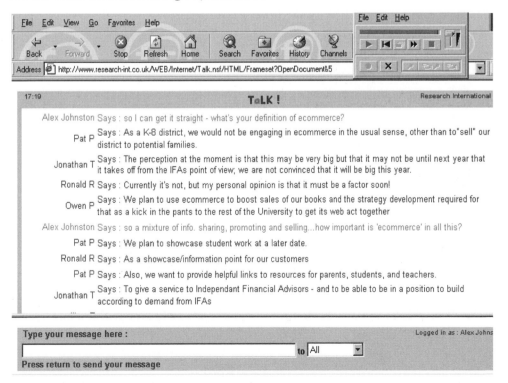

Figure 6.3: Online focus groups. *Source*: Research international/Crouch and Housden (2003)

Depth interviewees are recruited in the same way but the communication takes place simply between the respondent and the interviewer. The Web is not the ideal medium to deliver this type of research.

Problems with online interviews include:

◆ It is often hard to recruit suitable respondents.

◆ Technical knowledge is required to participate and a common technical platform is required. There are issues over the reliability of the Internet connection, and diverse browsers and so on. Respondents may view screens at different speeds, in different frame sizes and so on.

◆ Interaction is limited and body language cannot be seen although the use of web cams may help this.

◆ It is hard to interpret sarcastic comments other than through the use of emoticons, icons that express emotion, for example :-) or :-(.

◆ It is hard to maintain attention for long periods.

◆ It is a less creative environment for respondents.

◆ It is hard to moderate the contribution of all respondents.

◆ It is hard to establish who exactly is sitting at the terminal.

Advantages include the following:

◆ Bringing geographically dispersed samples together.

◆ It may be appropriate for B2B markets.

◆ It may be useful for e-commerce businesses.

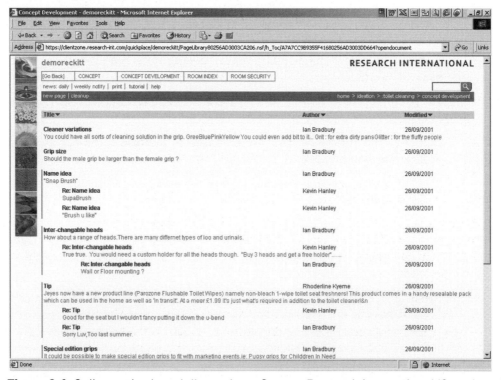

Figure 6.4: Online notice board discussions. *Source*: Research international/Crouch and Housden (2003)

Online depth interviews have similar disadvantages but depth interviews online are hard to sustain for more than 10 minutes.

There are some advantages especially in B2B markets where the use of online techniques may fit more easily with the respondents' work practices.

Analysis of qualitative data

The analysis of qualitative data is a skilled job and vital to get maximum value from the research. It is usual for the moderator or interviewer to carry out the analysis. The starting point is to organize the data, which is contained on tape. These tapes should always be kept. It may be that a written transcript of the tapes has to be made and this can take a significant amount of time, but is nearly always needed to enable effective analysis.

The analysis should enable the broad themes discussed during the research to be explored. We are looking for areas of agreement and disagreement, looking to reflect the range of views held and whether these views were strongly held. We may be trying to report on underlying behaviour and attitudes. Where stimuli have been used, these should be presented in the report and the output analysed.

Organizing the data

Wilson (2006) suggests four methods for data organization:

◆ **Tabular** – In which data is organized according to certain characteristics or themes. The content from the groups or interviews is then divided into these areas. This can be done on spreadsheets or within word processing packages.

◆ **Cut and paste** – Material is physically cut from transcript and pasted into separate thematic sections.

◆ **Spider diagrams or mind maps** – Places the material at the centre of a diagram with responses emanating from the centre.

◆ **Annotation** – The researcher colour codes or annotates the transcript to bring together common themes.

Computer-based analysis

There are a number of computer systems that help qualitative researchers in their tasks. Content analysis software counts the number of times a word or phrase appears in a transcript. This can help in initial analysis but tends to be a bit flat and gives a feel for the data but little more.

Text analysis or theory building software is more advanced in that it attaches codes to categories of statements and groups them together. This can help significantly in organizing data but still does not help in its interpretation, in which the skills of analysis and contextualization are combined with instinct and gut feel and these remain paramount.

The leading suppliers of qualitative data analysis software are QSR. They supply two main packages – Nvivo and XSight. Look at their website at www.qsrinternational.com.

Summary

In this unit we looked at the area of qualitative research. We saw that among other definitions, it can be defined as 'Research that is undertaken using an unstructured research approach with a small number of carefully selected individuals to produce non-quantifiable insights into behaviour motivations and attitudes' (Wilson, 2006).

We saw that the essential characteristics of qualitative research are as follows:

◆ It is unquantifiable and it is not representative of larger populations.

◆ Data collection techniques are unstructured.

◆ It involves small samples of individuals or groups of people.

◆ It seeks to reveal opinions, motivations and attitudes.

We looked at the various data collection methods that are used in this area including focus groups, depth interviews and projective techniques. We looked at the advantages and disadvantages of each technique.

We looked in detail at the skills required of moderators/interviewers. They should be:

◆ Highly qualified and experienced in research and, possibly, psychology.

◆ Business and marketing aware. They need to be able to translate respondents' feelings into business advantage for their clients.

◆ Strong communicators, able to relate to a range of people.

◆ Hard to place regionally in terms of socio-economic class.

◆ Socially able, relaxed and friendly, but strong enough to control a room of animated, or conversely, disinterested respondents.

◆ Flexible and quick thinking, with the ability to respond to the unexpected.

We saw that the topic guide is a route map and timetable for both group and depth interviews and that the guide should break the interview into three distinct phases:

1 The introduction phase

2 The discussion phase

3 The summarizing phase.

We looked at the advantages of focus groups:

◆ They replicate the dynamic social interactions that occur in the marketplace.

◆ They provide rich and detailed knowledge of a subject.

◆ They are more efficient in terms of time. One focus group can be done in a day. Fourteen depth interviews might take at least two weeks to complete.

◆ They are cheaper per interviewee than depth interviews.

◆ They allow interaction with physical stimuli, for example products.

◆ They can involve multiple techniques within the framework of the focus group.

The advantages of depth interviews were also discussed:

◆ They are conducted face to face, and body language can be interpreted.

◆ Proximity may encourage respondents to reveal more than they might in a remote interview.

◆ The respondent is the centre of attention and can be probed at length to explore issues that the researcher feels are important. This is the annoying child syndrome with the researcher asking 'why?' (but more subtly) until the issue is explored adequately.

◆ Group dynamics may prevent individuals expressing themselves particularly over areas that are sensitive, like income.

◆ Recruitment tends to be easier.

◆ The logistics are easier, no special rooms are needed.

◆ They reveal depth of understanding.

◆ They are flexible. The line of questioning may evolve within the interview and between interviews.

◆ They can involve a range of techniques.

We explored the use of projective techniques and saw that these techniques can be revealing and interesting to administer. Techniques included:

◆ Sentence completion

◆ Story completion

◆ Word association

◆ Cartoon completion

◆ Mood boards

◆ Brand personality or brand CVs

◆ Brand mapping

◆ Thematic apperception tests or TAT tests

◆ Photo sorts

◆ Role play.

We explored the online applications of qualitative research. We saw that there are problems in carrying out qualitative work online. These included:

◆ It is often hard to recruit suitable respondents.

◆ Technical knowledge is required to participate, and a common technical platform is required.

◆ Interaction is limited and body language cannot be seen.

◆ It is hard to interpret the meaning of words without the tone of voice and body language.

◆ It is hard to maintain attention for long periods.

◆ It is a less creative environment for respondents.

◆ It is hard to moderate the contribution of all respondents.

◆ It is hard to establish who exactly is sitting at the terminal.

Finally we looked at the techniques for analysing the data, both offline and using the computer packages that are available. We saw that there are several ways of organizing qualitative data:

◆ Tabular

◆ Cut and paste

◆ Spider diagrams or mind maps

◆ Annotation.

Bibliography

Crouch, S. and Housden, M. (2003) *Marketing Research for Managers*, Oxford: Elsevier Butterworth-Heinemann, 3rd edition

Wilson, A. (2006) *Marketing Research: An Integrated Approach*, FT Prentice Hall, 2nd edition

Websites

AMR (2003) www.asiamarketresearch.com/asia/news.php

ESOMAR (2008) www.esomar.org

MRS (2005) www.mrs.org

Unit 7 Quantitative data

Table 7.1: Learning outcomes and knowledge and skills requirements

Learning outcomes	Knowledge and skills requirements
4.4 Identify and evaluate the various techniques for collecting quantitative data	Face to face survey methods Telephone interviews Postal surveys Online surveys
4.5 Identify and evaluate the various techniques for undertaking experimentation	Omnibus surveys Forum voting (pressing voting buttons) Hall tests Placement tests Simulated test markets

Study guide

This unit should take around two hours to complete.

Quantitative data – Research which seeks to make measurements as distinct from qualitative research (MRS, 2007).

CAPI – Computer aided personal interviewing.

CAWI – Computer aided web interviewing.

CATI – Computer aided telephone interviewing.

Surveys – 'The systematic collection, analysis and interpretation of information about some aspect of study. In market research, the term is applied particularly to the collection of information by means of sampling and interviews with the selected individuals' (MRS, 2007).

Omnibus surveys – 'A survey covering a number of topics, usually for different clients. The samples tend to be nationally representative and composed of types of people for which there is a general demand. Clients are charged by the market research agency on the basis of the questionnaire space or the number of questions' (MRS, 2007).

Postal surveys – Self-administered surveys are delivered to the respondents who then complete the questionnaire and return it.

Telephone interviewing – Interviews carried out using the telephone.

Face-to-face interviews – These are interviews that are carried out with respondents in face-to-face contact with the interviewer. Results are recorded on paper or digitally on a personal digital assistant, palmtop or laptop computer.

Introduction

Quantitative data is the best known currency of marketing research. It is quantitative data that gives us the opinion polls or allows companies to claim that nine out of ten customers prefer their product. It is quantifiable because data is collected in a way that allows generalizations to be made about a general population from taking a sample of that population. We will deal with this later.

In this unit we are going to look at how data is collected, exploring the principal methods of data collection and their application.

What is quantitative data?

The MRS (2007) defines quantitative data as 'Research which seeks to make measurements as distinct from qualitative research'.

Wilson (2006) defines quantitative research as 'research that is undertaken using a structured research approach with a sample of the population to produce quantifiable insights into behaviour motivations and attitudes'.

Wilson (2006) identifies five key characteristics of quantitative data:

1   Data gathering is more structured.

2   Research involves larger samples than qualitative research.

3   The data gathered can provide answers that will quantify the incidence of particular behaviour motivations and attitudes in the population under consideration.

4   Studies can be more easily replicated and direct comparisons can be made between studies.

5   Analysis is statistical in nature and will usually be done with the help of computer software.

Survey methods

Surveys are defined by the MRS (2007) as 'The systematic collection, analysis and interpretation of information about some aspect of study. In market research, the term is applied particularly to the collection of information by means of sampling and interviews with the selected individuals.'

In this unit we are looking at the first element of this definition, that is the collection of data. There are many ways of gathering research data in a structured way and almost every medium is capable of delivering research questions. These media have a range of capabilities and strengths and weaknesses relating to them. As a CIM delegate, you will need to understand the range of data collection methods used and the relative strengths and weaknesses of these methodologies.

The two broadest categories are self-completion and interviewer-administered surveys.

Within interviewer-administered surveys we can see that they can be delivered:

◆   Face-to-face

◆   Online

◆   Over the telephone

◆   A combination of the above.

Self administered surveys cover:

◆   Online or e-mail surveys

◆   Postal, fax or hand delivered surveys.

We will start with interviewer-administered surveys.

Face-to-face interviews

These are interviews that are carried out with respondents in face-to-face contact with the interviewer; results are recorded on paper or digitally on a personal digital assistant, palmtop or laptop computer.

These can be distinguished from interviewer-administered surveys that are carried out remotely via the telephone or a 'help me' button on a web page.

Insight: Marks for Marks

Marks and Spencer use face-to-face interviewing for evaluating consumer reaction to the store experience. Interviewers can approach respondents as they leave the store when the experience of the store is fresh in their minds. This allows for immediate reactions to be assessed without the respondents relying on their memory. The interviewer can interpret body language and probe to elicit real understanding.

Face-to-face interviewing also allows for a range of prompts to be used. These may be pack shots or lists of brands to stimulate customer responses.

The advantages of face-to-face contact methods are many:

◆ There is greater acceptance of the validity of the research if an interviewer can introduce the reasons for the research and show professional membership cards.

◆ The interview process is more efficient as non-eligible respondents can be screened out more effectively.

◆ They improve response rates as the interviewer can answer questions or help with any difficulty in completing the questionnaire.

◆ Personal contact creates a sense of obligation and this can be useful with long surveys. This can reduce the incidence of incomplete or unfinished interviews.

◆ Complexity can be introduced into the survey – for example, the use of show cards or other stimuli material is more easily managed.

◆ Empathy and encouragement can enable deeper consideration of the questions and ensure accuracy of some claims – for example, gender and age.

There are some disadvantages:

◆ Costs, particularly in B2B research, may be high, but this must be offset against a higher response rate.

◆ It can take a considerable amount of time to complete a survey.

◆ Interviewers may be demotivated and may take short cuts to ensure that their quota of completed surveys is made.

◆ Interview bias is a problem. Bias may affect:

  ◆ Who is interviewed – interviewers may select those who want to be interviewed. An Australian researcher used to do all his interviews on the beach at Bondi.

  ◆ The way questions are asked – with a negative inflection or a preceding ad-libbed comment 'I know this sounds stupid but ...'

  ◆ The way an interviewer responds verbally and visually to an answer – a raised eyebrow or an expression of shock is not required!

  ◆ The way an answer is recorded, the interpretation of a response may be biased.

◆ Safety of interviewing staff may be an issue in some areas.

◆ The training and control of field staff is important and adds to costs.

◆ A geographically dispersed sample, for example, regional store managers, is clearly difficult to administer in this way and other data collection methods might need to be considered.

Insight: The Interviewer Quality Control Scheme

The Market Research Society operates a scheme to ensure the quality of fieldwork. The Interviewer Quality Control Scheme aims to institute and maintain quality fieldwork. In 2005, 64 companies were members of the scheme. The scheme covers:

1 Consumer, social and qualitative research

2 Consumer and retail panels, and audits

3 Hall tests

4 Telephone research.

The scheme lays down minimum standards for recruitment, office procedures, supervision, training, quality control (IQCS standards are in line with BS 5750) and survey administration.

Each member company is visited annually by an independent inspector, and required to produce documentation and other evidence that it conforms to or exceeds the minimum standards.

The IQCS lays down standards for the checking of interviewers' work: 'A minimum of 10% of the sample is validated (5% for telephone centres who validate by remote listening in). A systematic, representative method is used for selecting individuals and a substantial proportion of their work is checked' (IQCS 2008).

Inspection can be made with a minimum of 24 hours' notice. If accepted as a member of the scheme, this is shown in the Market Research Society listing of organizations and providing market research services, in the *Research Buyer's Guide*. Members of the IQCS are also listed in its own annual handbook, *IQCS Minimum Service Standards for Market Research Data Collection*.

That booklet and full details of the IQCS standards will be sent on request by IQCS. E-mail: gwareing@lineone.net, or you can visit the website at www.iqcs.org

In-home or doorstep interviews

These are interviews carried out at the home of the respondent. These may be important if the sample is determined by postcode or type of dwelling. They have the advantage of putting the respondent at their ease but are generally hard to manage; and with the number of women in paid employment outside the home, their value in terms of ensuring access is reduced.

Street interviews

These are perhaps the most visible forms of marketing research. Respondents describe their mixed feelings on seeing the smiling face of the interviewer approaching them.

Street interviewing has a number of advantages:

◆ They are less expensive than home interviews.

◆ They allow respondents who conform to quota specifications to be identified and approached – for example, women with children or older men.

Disadvantages include:

◆ Some shopping centres charge a fee or do not allow researchers to interview customers.

◆ Respondents are unlikely to stop in the open air if it is raining.

◆ Interviews need to be as short as possible.

◆ There are many distractions to the respondent – for example, children or friends who are impatient.

Executive interviewing

This involves interviewing business people at their place of work. It is expensive and time-consuming. As for depth interviews, researchers must be knowledgeable and access may be difficult over a dispersed sample. Generally for B2B interviews, alternative data collection methods are more appropriate.

Others

Other types of face-to-face interviewing do exist. These may take place in other public places, for example in galleries or on buses and trains.

What makes a good interviewer?

From the above, it is clear that the weak point in the collection of survey data is often the interviewer.

Gender

The majority are women. At the risk of sounding sexist, there are several reasons for this: part-time work – interviewing is flexible and fits around other responsibilities. Women tend to have better listening skills and find it easier to elicit information from respondents.

Age

The ideal age requirements for entry to consumer interviewing is between 25 and 45 years. In B2B markets, older, more experienced interviewers may be required.

Social background

It is useful if the interviewer is not obviously from any social class. It helps if the interviewer has the ability to be 'chameleon-like' so as to be able to fit in with the respondent. Politically, interviewers should be aware but not activists. It is usual, when interviewers are recruited, for them to be screened for political activity if they are likely to be employed in asking political questions.

Education

Interviewers should be numerate and literate. They should have at least GCSE level English and Maths. In certain B2B projects it may be useful to have some business education.

Experience

Some experience of dealing with people and B2B interviewing experience in the sector under review may be desirable. Training in research interviewing is not vital but IQCS accredited interviewers are required to be trained. MRS training is available via the Accredited Interviewer Training Scheme. Interviewers are awarded the MRS Certificate in Interviewing Skills for Market & Social Research if they complete the MRS Accredited Interviewer Training Scheme. Information can be found at http://www.mrs.org.uk/training/aits.htm.

Personality

The ideal researcher is gregarious and outgoing but not overbearing. They should be a good listener capable of empathy. They should be capable of multitasking, that is listening and recording data simultaneously.

Computer Assisted Personal Interviewing (CAPI)

CAPI is conducted face to face, usually employing PDAs or laptop computers. The interviewer is prompted with the question by the computer and the appropriate response codes are keyed-in directly according to the respondent's answers. Routing procedures use these codes to determine which question appears next. Since the data is entered directly into the computer, analyses can be produced quickly (MRS, 2007). If these are connected to a mobile network, results can be uploaded immediately.

CAPI has a number of advantages:

◆ Data entry is much simpler.

◆ There is no print production, so it is cheaper.

◆ The computer can check for inconsistent replies – for example, if a respondent has said that he is a non-smoker and later tells an interviewer that he smokes three cigarettes a week on average.

The costs of face-to-face interviewing

Costs will vary according to the sector and method of data collection. Face-to-face interviews range between £20 and £50. According ESOMAR in 2007 about 12 per cent of research data was captured using face-to-face interviews methods.

Ensuring the quality of data

Interviewers, as we have said, can be the weak link in the chain. Membership of the IQCS should help ensure data quality but other factors need to be considered.

◆ **Good interviewer briefing** – Briefing sessions for interviews should introduce the object of the research, introduce the questionnaire, allow the interviewers to practise using the questionnaire and ask any questions.

◆ **Monitoring in the field** – Field force managers should observe interviewers and ensure that standards are maintained.

◆ **Back checking** – The IQCS insists that at least 10% of completed interviews.

◆ **Careful editing** – Ensuring that the data is consistent and complete.

◆ **Good research design** – The questionnaire must be easy to use and efficient.

A checklist for employing a fieldwork agency

When employing a fieldwork agency, Crouch and Housden (2003) present the following checklist that may be used to ask the right questions:

◆ Is there a fieldwork manager?

◆ How many interviewers you have?

◆ How many supervisors are there?

◆ Do the supervisors work exclusively for this agency?

◆ What is the agency's supervisory structure, that is how many supervisors and how many interviewers per supervisor?

◆ How are interviewers selected?

◆ How are interviewers trained?

◆ On average, how long do interviewers stay with your organization?

◆ How many interviewers work exclusively for your agency?

◆ What quality control procedures are used?

Telephone interviewing

Telephone research involves interviewing respondents over the telephone. This may be done at home but more usually is managed via a call or contact centre. The use of the telephone in market research is growing. This is due to a number of factors:

◆ **Changing environment** – There is far greater acceptance of the telephone as a means of communication. Younger people are very comfortable on the telephone. It is common to see people using their mobile phones to talk to each other even when they are only 30 metres apart.

◆ **The way we work** – Telephone research mirrors many business processes and distribution networks. Business is changing. People are used to transacting over the telephone. Over 30 per cent of motor insurance policies are sold over the telephone.

Two per cent of the entire UK workforce is employed in the 'call centre' industry. This is more than mining, fishing and agriculture combined. The UK is the largest user of call centres in Europe employing 39 per cent of the total agents in Europe, and with 5000–16,000 call centres, depending on the definition used.

◆ With **legislation and de-regulation**, the market for telephone services has opened up and cost of calls has fallen.

◆ **Mobile phones** and mobile Internet access mean that research can use a range of methods to reach and stimulate respondents.

◆ **Technology enables very efficient calling procedures** – These include computer telephony integration (CTI) linking the call centre to the marketing database, CATI systems, bespoke systems for the management of telephone research and interactive voice recognition (IVR) that enables calls to be made automatically.

Telephone interviewing has a number of advantages:

◆ The cost at around £10–20 per interview is lower than face-to-face interviewing. Larger surveys can be administered via a call centre far cheaper than this at around £5 per call. The use of automated research is more common in the United States but it is possible to run a research programme using voice recognition software.

◆ Control is much easier. The latest call centre software allows for calls and interviews to be recorded or monitored by research managers.

◆ Bias due to non-verbal influence is removed and verbal influence can be controlled through the monitoring process.

◆ It is very good for geographically dispersed samples. These can be accessed via the telephone without the need for the interviewer to travel, saving time and money.

◆ It is fast. We can see this during the election process. The research companies can produce statistically valid data within hours of a particular issue emerging.

◆ It is convenient for the interviewer and the respondent. Calls may be made that allow the interviewer to call back at a convenient time to deliver the interview.

◆ Third-generation mobile phones, mobile Internet access and SMS text messaging have extended the capability of the phone as a medium for data capture.

Disadvantages include:

◆ Generally the telephone has lower response rates than face-to-face interviews.

◆ Respondents find it easier to say 'no' on the telephone.

◆ They may screen their calls.

◆ They may be ex-directory.

◆ They may not engage fully with the interview process and fail to complete the questionnaire.

◆ Research design is restricted. The use of stimuli is limited even if the interview is carried out via mobile Internet access. The length of the interview has to be shorter than face-to-face interviews in order to maintain the interest of the respondent.

◆ Some social classes have a greater preponderance of ex-directory numbers.

◆ Access to mobile telephone numbers may be difficult to obtain.

◆ As the use of the telephone becomes ubiquitous, negative reaction to the use of the telephone becomes more common. The telephone is intrusive and the use of cold-calling by certain market sectors has created a problem for market researchers.

◆ In some international markets, issues of access might be a concern. Attitudes to the use of telephone in market research may be less positive than in the UK.

◆ Whilst marketing research is exempt from the conditions of the telephone preference service, response rates to telephone interviews can be an issue.

Computer assisted telephone interviewing (CATI)

It is defined by the MRS as 'computer assisted interviewing, over the telephone' (MRS, 2003). It can facilitate the design, administration and analysis of telephone interviewing.

Software such as SNAP can be used to design, deliver, analyse and report on surveys very effectively.

◆ Questionnaires can be customized and verbal comments can be recorded.

◆ Inconsistencies can be highlighted and the researcher can probe to correct them.

◆ Automated dialling allows for efficient management of the interviewer.

◆ It is more possible and may be used to capture simple research data, for example customer satisfaction data.

Web-based interviews

Whilst not strictly interviewer administered, the use of 'call me' or 'help me' buttons on Web-administered questionnaires allows a degree of interviewer assistance to take place. 'Help me' buttons allow a pop-up dialogue screen in which questions can be asked and answered. Whilst help line numbers might be included in other self-administered questionnaires the immediacy of the online environment is more conducive to this offer being taken up.

'Phone me' allows the respondent to be contacted by telephone and helped through the questionnaire. In some instances, it is possible for a contact centre to see the respondent's screen. Use of CAWI is helping this process and it adds significantly to the range of data that can be captured, for example, by self-eadministered surveys. These are delivered to the respondents who then complete the questionnaire and return it.

Self-completion surveys

There are several types of self-completion surveys. They are:

◆ Postal

◆ Fax

◆ Hand-delivered

◆ E-mail or Web-based.

Postal surveys

Postal surveys are used significantly within the research industry. They are mailed to respondents with a covering letter, a response device, usually a business reply envelope, and a questionnaire. Postal research is used in the direct marketing industry where the mechanism reflects the medium used to communicate with customers but it is popular throughout industry sectors.

It has several advantages:

◆ It is cheap; the cost can be as low as £5 per interview.

◆ It is useful for geographically dispersed and larger samples.

◆ It reduces interviewer bias as there is no interviewer asking the questions.

◆ Questionnaires can be piloted and revisions made. On large-scale samples, testing can lead to careful measurement of expected response rates.

◆ It is convenient for interviewees as the questionnaire can be completed at any time.

◆ The research design is limited but longer questionnaires can be delivered and completed effectively in this way.

◆ The use of self-completion allows respondents to confer and this may be desirable when researching high-involvement purchases.

There are disadvantages:

◆ Response rates may be low, sometimes as low as 1–2 per cent. They can be increased through time-limited incentives and appeals to a sense of duty – rates can then be as high as 50–60 per cent and sometimes even higher.

◆ Research design is limited.

◆ They may take time to complete and this can lead to low response.

◆ The availability of lists to form a sample frame may be limited in certain markets.

◆ There is limited control over the respondent and a higher incidence of incomplete questionnaires or inconsistent answers may be expected. This can be alleviated through good questionnaire design and careful piloting.

◆ There is potential for bias in responders as those who respond may be those who feel strongly about an issue.

Whilst postal survey response rates may be low, these can be increased by:

◆ **Prescreening** – Calls can be made to respondents prior to sending the questionnaire. This could confirm details and create a sense of expectation and commitment to the process.

◆ **Reminder calls** or letters to encourage the respondent to reply – these may take place at a specified time after the questionnaire has been sent. Some agencies will send duplicate copies of the research questionnaires.

◆ **Incentives** – In consumer markets, coupons or vouchers can be used; in B2B markets access to an executive summary of the final report may be offered as an incentive.

◆ **Personalizing the survey** – Postal research response rates tend to be higher when the research is part of an existing relationship. Data collection methods need to reflect the nature of the population under consideration.

The covering letter is crucial to introduce the research and the organization carrying out the research. It may contain a letter of reference or professional membership symbols.

Wilson (2006) suggests that the covering letter should contain:

◆ The purpose of the research

◆ Assurances of confidentiality

◆ Reasons why they should respond

♦ The time needed to complete the research

♦ A number and name for enquiries

♦ Time scales and manner of return

♦ Thanks.

Hand-delivered surveys

Questionnaires can be handed out or left for collection; for example, flight surveys or surveys left in hotel bedrooms or given to diners in restaurants. These can achieve high response rate, are cheap to administer but generally are hard to control and should be used carefully with support from other methods.

Fax surveys

Share similar strengths and weaknesses to postal surveys. A few years ago these were very popular, today they are less so. The development of e-mail and the Internet has superseded this technology that was used largely in B2B research. It can still be helpful to include fax-back as a way of returning a postal survey.

E-mail and web surveys

A growing area for research in both B2B and consumer markets, the range of methods using e-mail and the Internet is expanding very quickly. E-mail and web surveys are difficult to separate out as e-mail surveys may contain a link through to a website survey or they may include the questionnaire as an attachment to the e-mail or within the e-mail itself.

Online methods have a number of advantages:

♦ They are cheap to administer, design, deliver and analyse.

♦ They are flexible in content and can include image and sound files.

♦ They are fast to administer and to report on.

♦ They have immediate and low-cost global reach.

♦ They can replicate customer behaviour in both consumer and business markets.

♦ They can appear automatically as pop-ups, as a browser scrolls over a certain part of a page. Dell use this system on their website – a service designed by Opinionlabs (www.opinionlabs.com).

♦ They are easy to control.

♦ They can be completed at the respondents' convenience.

There are several disadvantages:

♦ Technology is varied and the use of attachments or HTML e-mails may not be supported by all computers.

♦ The amount of unsolicited e-mails may affect perception of the questionnaire.

♦ Samples might be difficult to construct as e-mail lists are not very reliable and there is limited access to the Internet and e-mail – especially in the lower socio-economic groups and in certain international markets.

◆ It may be hard to validate who has responded as anyone could be using the computer.

◆ People remain suspicious of the Internet and confidentiality needs to be ensured.

◆ There may be a cost to the respondent especially if the questionnaire takes time to download.

◆ The ease of use in some organizations has led to very poor 'research' being carried out on an ad-hoc basis.

Omnibus surveys

Omnibus surveys are defined by the MRS (2007) as 'A survey covering a number of topics, usually for different clients. The samples tend to be nationally representative and composed of types of people for which there is a general demand. Clients are charged by the market research agency on the basis of the questionnaire space or the number of questions required.'

Wilson (2006) defines omnibus surveys as a 'Data collection approach that is undertaken at regular intervals for a changing group of clients who share the costs involved in the survey's set up sampling and interviewing.'

Crouch and Housden (2003) define omnibus research as 'Research surveys which are undertaken with a stated frequency and a decided method, using a set number of respondents and sampling points.'

Omnibus surveys represent a halfway house between secondary and primary research. For the user, it gives access to low-cost primary data that is representative and fast to report on. The user pays only for the questions asked, but has no control over question order or sequencing.

Omnibus surveys have a number of advantages:

◆ They are cheap, typically a simple question can be placed for around £1200, more complex questions will cost more.

◆ Quantified analysis can be accessed extremely quickly.

◆ Representative of a market and statistically valid.

◆ Gives access to 'hard to research' markets – for example, directors or small business owners.

Disadvantages:

◆ The sample cannot be changed.

◆ Questions must be phrased simply.

◆ Not suitable for opinions or attitudes.

◆ Question order may affect responses.

The *Research Buyer's Guide* identifies suppliers of omnibus surveys and there is a useful section on this in *Marketing Research for Managers*, one of your course texts.

There are two types of omnibus research. General omnibus surveys represent the entire adult population and specialist surveys cover sectors, for example motorist or gardeners.

According to Wilson (2006), when choosing an omnibus supplier you should consider the following aspects:

◆ The population covered

◆ Data collection methods

◆ Frequency of fieldwork

◆ Reputation of the supplier

◆ Speed of reporting

◆ Sample size and composition.

Other methods

Hall tests

Hall tests are defined by the MRS as 'A group of respondents are recruited to attend a fixed location, often a large room or hall, where they respond – usually as individuals – to a set of stimuli'.

Hall tests can be used to evaluate new products, designs and creative propositions. These stimuli can be tested on their own, known as monadic tests, or in comparison with others, known as multiple tests.

Hall tests are usually carried out in a number of locations and typically 100–400 respondents will be interviewed.

Placement tests

This involves placing products in the home. Respondents use the product and then complete a questionnaire on it. Two or more products may be compared at the same time or different products may be compared sequentially.

Simulated test markets

Simulated test markets have, to some extent, replaced traditional test marketing. The process is as follows:

◆ Participants are recruited who are representative of the target market.

◆ They are exposed to marketing stimuli in the sector including the new product.

◆ Participants are given the opportunity to buy from a range of products in a catalogue held by the researcher, using their own money.

◆ Any follow-n purchases must be from the researcher.

◆ This data is then modelled to produce a picture of the roll-out of the new product.

Panels

Panels are defined by the MRS (2007) as 'A permanent representative sample maintained by a market research agency from which information is obtained on more than one occasion either for continuous research or for ad hoc projects.'

Panels cover a range of market sectors and can be identified via the MRS website and the *Research Buyer's Guide*. They can be used to ensure that data can be gathered quickly or on a continuous basis. We looked at panels in Unit 4 on observation.

The key requirements for setting up panels are:

◆ Recruitment

◆ Retention

◆ Replacement.

Panels exist in a range of sectors and include online shoppers, media behaviour and consumption patterns in a range of markets.

Forum voting and deliberative events

Forum voting is a research technique in which members of a forum can vote for their preferred option. The technique has been used, for example, in public sector planning and in political marketing. There are emerging data capture techniques which allow for a hybrid approach to research. Deliberative events, for example, may capture quantitative data using voting buttons but also include elements of qualitative discussion groups.

The Department for Business, Enterprise and Regulatory Reform (BERR) recently ran a series of deliberative events to discuss the future of nuclear power in the UK.

Forums are run often in sports centres and theatres and may include over 100 participants at a time. There are a range of inputs and activities and the aim is to produce a high-energy engaging experience that allows for a range of insights to be captured. GfK NOP have run these forums both live and using second life scenarios in an online environment.

Summary

In this unit we looked at the methods of collecting data for quantitative research.

Quantitative research was defined as 'research that is undertaken using a structured research approach with a sample of the population to produce quantifiable insights into behaviour motivations and attitudes' (Wilson, 2006).

We saw that data gathering is more structured, and is made from larger samples. This enables quantitative analysis and comparable studies to be carried out.

We looked in detail at data collection methods, including interviewer-administered questionnaires and self-completion questionnaires.

Interviewer-administered methods included face-to-face, telephone- and Web-based questionnaires. Self-completion included postal, fax, e-mail and web questionnaires.

We saw that face-to-face data collection had a number of advantages:

◆ There is greater acceptance of the validity of the research if an interviewer can introduce the reasons for the research and show professional membership cards.

◆ The interview process is more efficient as non-eligible respondents can be screened out more effectively.

- They improve response rates as the interviewer can answer questions or help with any difficulty in completing the questionnaire.

- Personal contact creates a sense of obligation and this can be useful with long surveys. This can reduce the incidence of incomplete or unfinished interviews.

- Complexity can be introduced into the survey – for example, the use of show cards or other stimuli material is more easily managed.

- Empathy and encouragement can enable deeper consideration of the questions and ensure accuracy of some claims – for example, gender and age.

There were also some disadvantages:

- Costs particularly in B2B research may be high, but this must be offset against a higher response rate.

- It can take a considerable amount of time to complete a survey.

- Interviewers may be demotivated and may take short cuts to ensure that their quota of completed surveys is made.

- Interview bias is a problem. Bias may affect:
  - Who is interviewed
  - The way questions are asked
  - The way an interviewer responds verbally and visually to an answer
  - The way an answer is recorded.

- Safety of interviewing staff may be an issue in some areas.

- The training and control of field staff is important and adds to costs.

- A sample dispersed geographically, for example, regional store managers, is clearly difficult to administer in this way and other data collection methods might need to be considered.

- Face-to-face interviews may be carried out:
  - In the home
  - In the street
  - In the office (executive interviews)
  - In other public places.

We looked at the personal qualities of good interviewers and at the IQCS as a means for ensuring quality of fieldwork.

We went on to look at CAPI and its advantages:

- Data entry is much simpler.

- There is no print production, so it is cheaper.

- The computer can check for inconsistent replies – for example, a respondent has said that he is a non-smoker and later tells an interviewer he smokes on average three cigarettes a week.

The telephone is one of the fastest growing media for collecting data. We looked at the reasons for this:

- ◆ Changing environment.
- ◆ Telephone research mirrors many business processes and distribution networks.
- ◆ Mobile phones and mobile Internet access means that research can use a range of methods to reach and stimulate respondents.
- ◆ Technology enables very efficient calling procedures.

We looked at the advantages and disadvantages of using the telephone.

Advantages:

- ◆ The cost
- ◆ Control
- ◆ It is very good for international or other geographically dispersed samples
- ◆ It is fast
- ◆ It is convenient
- ◆ Third-generation mobile phones, mobile Internet access and SMS text messaging have extended the capability of the phone as a medium for data capture.

Disadvantages:

- ◆ Lower response rates.
    - ◆ Respondents find it easier to say 'no' on the telephone.
    - ◆ They may screen their calls.
    - ◆ They may be ex-directory.
    - ◆ They may not engage fully with the interview process and fail to complete the questionnaire.
- ◆ Research design is restricted.
- ◆ Some social classes have a greater preponderance of ex-directory numbers.
- ◆ Access to mobile telephone numbers may be difficult to obtain.
- ◆ It is intrusive and may be irritating.
- ◆ In certain cases international access might be a concern.
- ◆ Attitudes to the use of telephone in market research may be less positive than in the United Kingdom.

We examined CATI and its advantages. These were:

- ◆ CATI can facilitate the design administration and analysis of telephone interviewing.
- ◆ Questionnaires can be customized and verbal comments can be recorded.
- ◆ Inconsistencies can be highlighted and the researcher can probe to correct the inconsistency.
- ◆ Automated dialling allows for efficient management of the interviewer.
- ◆ Completely automated telephone interviews are more practicable and may be used to capture simple research data, for example customer satisfaction data.

We saw that Web-based interviews could be interviewer-aided and that the use of CAWI is helping this process.

Self-administered surveys are ones that are delivered to the respondents who then complete the questionnaire and return them, and covered postal, hand-delivered, fax and e-mail or web questionnaires.

We looked at each in turn discussing the advantages of each.

Postal surveys were seen to have several advantages:

◆ Cheap.

◆ It is useful for geographically dispersed and larger samples.

◆ It reduces interview bias.

◆ Questionnaires can be piloted and revisions made.

◆ It is very convenient.

◆ Longer questionnaires can be delivered and completed effectively.

◆ They allow respondents to confer and this may be desirable when researching high involvement purchases.

The disadvantages:

◆ Response rate may be low.

◆ Research design is limited.

◆ They may take time to complete and this can lead to low response.

◆ The availability of lists to form sample frames.

◆ There is limited control over the respondent.

◆ A high incidence of incomplete questionnaires or inconsistent answers may be expected.

◆ There is potential for bias in responders as those who respond may be those who feel strongly about an issue.

We looked briefly at fax and hand-delivered surveys, and in more depth at online surveys.

Online methods were seen to have a number of advantages:

◆ They are cheap to administer, design, deliver and analyse.

◆ They are flexible in content.

◆ They are fast to administer and to report on.

◆ They have immediate and low-cost global reach.

◆ They can replicate customer behaviour in both consumer and business markets.

◆ They can be used automatically.

◆ They are easy to control.

◆ They can be completed at the respondents' convenience.

There are several disadvantages:

◆ Technology may not be supported by all computers.

◆ The amount of unsolicited e-mails or spam may affect perception of the questionnaire.

◆ Samples might be difficult to construct.

◆ It may be hard to validate who has responded.

◆ People remain suspicious of the Internet and confidentiality must be ensured.

◆ There may be a cost to the respondent especially if the questionnaire takes time to download.

◆ The ease of use in some organizations has led to very poor 'research' being carried out on an ad-hoc basis.

Finally, we looked at omnibus surveys, hall tests and reviewed the use of panel data.

Omnibus surveys were seen to have the following advantages:

◆ Cheap

◆ Fast

◆ Representative

◆ Flexible.

Disadvantages:

◆ The sample cannot be changed.

◆ Questions must be phrased simply.

◆ Not suitable for opinions or attitudes.

◆ Question order may affect responses.

Finally, we looked at hall tests, simulated test markets, placement and panel data.

Bibliography

Crouch, S. and Housden, M. (2003) *Marketing Research for Managers*, Oxford: Elsevier Butterworth-Heinemann, 3rd edition

Wilson, A. (2006) *Marketing Research: An Integrated Approach*, FT Prentice Hall, 2nd edition

Websites

AMA (2007) www.marketingpower.com

ESOMAR (2008) www.ESOMAR.org

MRS (2007) www.mrs.org.uk

Unit 8 Sampling

Table 8.1: Learning outcomes and knowledge and skills requirements

Learning outcomes	Knowledge and skills requirements
4.6 Explain and evaluate different sampling approaches	The sampling process Difference between probability and non-probability samples Knowledge of convenience, judgement and quota samples Determining sample size Sampling and non-sampling error Panels

Key definitions

Sample – A part or subset of a population taken to be representative of the whole.

Sampling frame – A list of the population of interest from which the sample in a survey is drawn.

Population – The total number of people in any defined group of interest.

Census – A survey of the entire population.

Sample element – An individual member of the sample frame.

Confidence level – The probability that the true population value will fall within a known range.

Probability sampling – A sampling method that uses objective sample selection so that every member of a population has a known probability of being selected.

Cluster sampling – A procedure in which clusters of population units are selected at random and then all or some of the units in the chosen clusters are studied.

Non-probability sampling – Non-probability sampling involves a subjective selection of respondents. Therefore, the probability of selecting respondents is unknown. This means that because the sample is not chosen objectively it is not possible to state results with any degree of statistical certainty.

Quota sampling – A sampling method that selects a sub-sample based on known proportions in the population.

Convenience sampling – Based on the convenience of the researcher. It may be that the section is made in the street, in the office or from a database. As long as the sample fits with the population as a whole, it is legitimate.

Judgement or purposive sampling – The researcher consciously selects a sample considered appropriate for the study.

Sample error – The error in a survey caused by using a sample to estimate the value of a parameter in the population.

Simple random sampling – A probability sampling method in which respondents are selected using random numbers.

Systematic sampling – A probability sampling method in which respondents are selected using a '1 in n' approach.

Stratified random sampling – A probability sampling method in which the sample is forced to contain respondents from each of the key segments of a population.

Standard deviation – A measurement of dispersion that calculates the average distance of the values in a data set from the mean value.

Snowball sampling – A type of non-probability sampling where initial respondents are selected at random and subsequent respondents are then selected by referrals or information from the earlier respondents.

Study guide

This unit of the coursebook will take you two hours to complete.

Introduction

This unit is concerned with the process of deciding which individuals will be asked to provide information. It is very unusual for an entire population to be surveyed. A population refers to the total number of people in a group of interest. One of the few examples of this is the 10-year census in the UK. Rather as a chef tastes his food in order to determine the taste of the entire dish, so the market researcher seeks the views of a sample of the population under consideration. However, the market researcher must also ensure that all the ingredients have been used and that the ingredients have been correctly mixed.

Key to the accuracy of this is the determination of the characteristics of the sample. Wilson (2006) highlights five key questions that inform the sampling process:

1   We need to understand the nature of the people we wish to survey.

2   We need to know where they are.

3   We need to know how we select them.

4   We need to know the number of people we wish to survey.

5   We need to know how representative this sample is of the population as a whole.

This unit outlines the process involved in creating a valid sample for research purposes.

What is a sample?

Crouch and Housden (2003) define a sample as:

A small number taken from a large group for testing and analysis, on the assumption that the sample is representative of the population as a whole.

The MRS (2007) defines a sample as:

A part or subset of a population taken to be representative of the population as a whole for the investigative purposes of research.

Sampling is used to make an estimate of the characteristics of the population as a whole. It overcomes the impossibility in almost every population of asking all members their opinion.

◆   It is efficient.

◆   It is easier to manage.

◆   It is cheap.

◆   It is subject to statistical verification.

◆   It allows for a high degree of precision.

The sampling process

Wilson (2006) outlines a six-stage sampling process (Figure 8 .1).

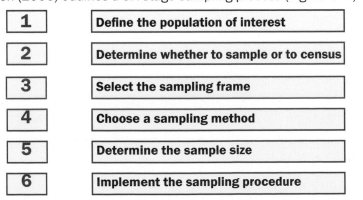

Figure 8.1: The sampling process. *Source:* Wilson 2006

Define the population of interest

Samples are selected from populations. The population is the total number of individuals in the group in which we are interested. This may be established at any level. We may be interested in all car dealers, we may be interested in Renault dealers, or we may be interested in Renault dealers in London and the south-east.

The definition of the population of interest is of vital importance. It is possible that the definition will produce a very low number of people in the sample. This has implications that we will explore below.

The key thing is that the definition of the population informs the whole research process. It will determine the methodology, the nature of questions asked and the interview process. The interviewer will be given screening criteria on which to select and deselect potential respondents.

For example, 'Women living in Essex who are working, and who have applied for child tax relief in the last three months'.

Some people in the defined population will be deselected by virtue of other characteristics. They work in market research and are employed by the Benefits Agency or Inland Revenue.

Sample or census?

Remember the difference? A census covers the entire population; a sample is a part of that population. It is unusual for a census to take place unless the population is small. This may take place in certain B2B markets – for example, regional distributors of industrial machinery. Here the population is small and a census is appropriate. However, it is more usual that the population may include thousands or millions of individuals – for example, supermarket shoppers, voters or council tax payers.

Selecting the sample frame

The ESOMAR (2007) defines the sampling frame as 'A list of the population of interest that is used to draw the sample in a survey, for example a telephone directory or a list of members of a profession.'

Sample frames are used to select the individual who will be interviewed. It is important that the frame reflects the characteristics of the population and a number of lists may need to be combined to ensure this. Wilson (2006) points out that a telephone directory may not include all elements of a population, for example those who are ex-directory, those who use a mobile phone or those with no telephone. This is known as sample frame error.

If there is no suitable list, a list of the general population may be used and classification questions used to select respondents who fit the population of interest.

Let's look at an example. If you had been commissioned to conduct research into marketing directors of companies involved in food and drinks production in the United Kingdom the sample frame may be developed from the following lists:

◆ The members' list of the CIM, MRS or IDM

◆ Members of the Institute of Directors

◆   Companies' House

◆   Subscriber lists to the marketing press

◆   Business directory services such as Kompass

◆   Business-to-business profiling companies like Dunn and Bradstreet

◆   Trade association in the food and drinks sector

There are a number of other possibilities.

Choosing a sampling method

There are two broad sampling methods.

Probability sampling

The key characteristic is that every member of the population of interest has a known chance of being selected, independent of any subjective selection by the researcher. For example, each member of a sample frame is given a number, and respondents are randomly selected until the required sample is selected.

Advantages are that the results can be projected onto the population as a whole subject to a known sampling error. This means that we can identify the limits of error for any particular result. For example, a research report might state that results are correct at the 95 per cent confidence level ±3 per cent.

What does this mean?

First that the sample has a 1 in 20 chance of being wrong, and secondly that a result of say 45 per cent actually will fall between 48 and 42 per cent, that is 45 + 3 or 45 – 3.

It should be clear that when a small sample is used to reflect the views of a population this calculation can only be approximate. The larger the sample, the greater confidence we can have that the sample will reflect accurately the population as a whole and the closer its views will be to the population as a whole. We will look at this in detail later.

Of course the way that respondents are selected adds to the cost of the survey.

Non-probability sampling

Non-probability sampling involves a subjective selection of respondents. Therefore, the probability of selecting respondents is unknown. This means that because the sample is not chosen objectively it is not possible to state results with any degree of statistical certainty.

Non-probability sampling has advantages and disadvantages.

Advantages:

◆   Lower cost

◆   Faster

◆   Smaller sample sizes

◆   Important respondents can be targeted.

Disadvantages:

◆ Results are purely indicative.

◆ Sampling error cannot be computed.

◆ The degree of representativeness of the sample to the population is not known.

◆ Assumptions need to be made about the groupings with the population of interest.

Probability sampling

There are four commonly used methods of probability sampling:

(a) Simple random sampling

(b) Systematic sampling

(c) Stratified random sampling

(d) Cluster sampling.

Simple random sampling

Each member of the population has an equal chance of being selected for the survey. Members are randomly selected by a computerized random number generator or tables until the required sample size is filled.

Probability of selection is worked out as population size divided by the required sample size. For example if we require a sample of 500 and the population of interest is 20,000 the probility of selection is 40.

Systematic sampling

This is easier than random sampling as it does not use random number generation. In the previous activity, we looked at a sample size of 500 from a population of 20,000. In systematic random sampling, the figure of 40 would be used as what is known as a skip interval and every 40th name would be selected from the list.

Stratified random sampling

This method divides the population into two or more mutually exclusive groups – for example, men or women, users or non-users of a product – and takes random samples from within them using either of the methods above.

This can be done proportionately where potential respondents or units are selected in proportion to the total number in each subset or disproportionately which takes more units from the subset with fewer respondents, that is where there is greater variation.

Whilst the disproportionate method is efficient and reliable, the proportionate method is more commonly used as the researcher may not know in advance the level of diversity within each subset.

Cluster sampling

Cluster sampling is described by Wilson (2006) as:

A procedure in which clusters of population units are selected at random and then all or some of the units in the chosen clusters are studied.

The technique works by identifying clusters within a population and selecting randomly from these clusters. The technique works when a population can easily be divided into representative clusters, for example in membership directories.

Disadvantages include the difficulty of forming a mini version of the population which maintains the characteristics of the population as a whole. Rather like Dr Evil and Mini Me, the characteristics may change and may be hard to control!!

Wilson (2006) identifies three approaches to cluster sampling:

1 **One-stage** – Clusters are selected randomly and data is gathered from all people in the clusters.

2 **Two-stage** – Clusters are selected randomly and data is gathered for a random sample of people in the selected clusters.

3 **Area sampling** – Geographical clusters are created and a random sample of individuals is selected.

Multi-stage sampling

This is a method which has several advantages. The chief is to concentrate a dispersed sample into convenient locations.

For example in surveying UK households, a random selection of constituencies might be made, this would be followed by a random selection of wards, then polling districts and finally a selection of streets and then individuals.

Advantages include the fact that the creation of the sample frame is easier and the final interviews end up being geographically clustered reducing costs of face-to-face interviews.

Limitations of random sampling

◆ It is expensive.

◆ Respondents selected must be interviewed to ensure the integrity of the process. This means that up to three call-backs to individuals may be made before classifying them as non-responses.

◆ The cost of pulling together a large sample frame may be prohibitive.

◆ The random selection of a sample means that all members of a national population would have the same chance of being selected. This means that interviewers may have to cover Land's End to John o'Groats.

Non-probability sampling

There are four types of non-probability sampling.

Convenience sampling

It is based on the convenience for the researcher. It may be that the section is made in the street, in the office or from a database. As long as the sample fits with the population as a whole, it is legitimate.

Judgement or purposive sampling

The researcher consciously selects a sample considered appropriate for the study. This may be based on certain companies representing a sector – for example, a researcher in the cutlery market might include all major department stores in the sample as well as a random selection of other outlets. This is designed to reflect the relative importance of department stores in the retail market.

Quota sampling

It is defined by ESOMAR (2007) as 'A type of non-probability sample where the required number of units with particular characteristics are specified.' This is based on the idea that if known characteristics of the population are reproduced in the same proportion in the sample, it is representative of that population; for example, age, sex and social class can be used to select quotas.

A researcher may be required to interview an equal split of men and women and a certain number of men of a certain age. The researcher selects respondents that comply with the quota laid down (Figure 8.2).

Quota Category	Required	Achieved	Total
Male	100		
16-34	40		
35-54	40		
55+	20		
Socio-economic			
ABC1	40		
C2	35		
DE	25		

Figure 8.2: Quota sheets

Advantages include:

◆ Speed and cost.

◆ Allows sampling to take place where a sample frame may not be available but key characteristics of the population are known, e.g. in overseas B2B research.

◆ Interviewers do not have to interview named individuals; they are screened in or out via a small number of classification questions.

◆ The data, when compared to random methods which are perhaps double the cost, has been proved to be acceptable provided that the research is managed effectively.

◆ Cost savings may be used to improve the quality of research through increasing sample sizes or using a different method in support of the survey.

◆ Its popularity shows that it works!

Disadvantages include:

◆ Whilst known characteristics may be distributed in correct proportions, unknown characteristics that may be relevant to the survey may not be. Hidden bias may exist that is not discovered.

◆ Researchers may be biased as to the type of respondents they choose to interview or the location where they choose to carry out the interviews. A quota for young people may be filled at one youth club but will not be truly representative.

149

Snowball sampling

It is defined by ESOMAR (2007) as:

A type of non-probability sampling where initial respondents are selected at random and subsequent respondents are then selected by referrals or information from the earlier respondents.

This is very useful in markets where there is low incidence of the population – in B2B markets, where buyers are of competitive intelligence, or where unusual behaviour is under consideration.

Online issues

The same methods can be used in online research but the sample frames are less readily available. Panels have been set up to counter this, for example Nielsen net ratings.

Determining the sample size

There is no necessary relationship between the size of the population and the sample. Whilst the larger the sample size the more accurate the results, this has to be traded off against the cost of producing this effect and the complexity, and therefore cost of managing the collection and processing of large amounts of data.

The cost of producing a larger response is normally proportional, that is the percentage increase in the cost of producing a percentage increase in sample size will be the same. However, the increase in accuracy is not proportional. As Wilson (2006) points out, sampling error tends to decrease at a rate equal to the square root of the relative increase in sample size. A sample increased by 100 per cent will improve accuracy by 10 per cent.

Sample size is often determined by past experience. Previous studies will indicate:

◆ The degree of variability in the population – the more the variability, the larger the sample size will need to be.

◆ The likely response rates – if these are believed to be low, the sample will need to be larger.

◆ The incident rate of the characteristic being researched – if this is common, the sample may be smaller.

◆ The number of subgroups within the data – the smaller groups will have larger sampling errors and a larger sample might be needed to ensure that subgroups can be effectively analysed.

Other factors play a key role in determining sample size. These include:

◆ **Budget** – always a factor in marketing decisions; the higher the sample size, the greater the cost.

◆ **Timings** – the larger the sample size, the longer it takes to gather data and complete the analysis.

◆ **The risk attached to any decision** – the greater the risk, the higher the level of accuracy required.

The nature of the research may indicate complex analysis of subsamples, for example women as opposed to men buying a certain product; if this is the case the sub-samples need to be large enough to ensure statistical reliability.

Statistical techniques for determining sample size

For probability samples, statistical methods are used to establish sample sizes.

We need three pieces of information to work this out.

1   Variance and the degree of variability of the population, known as standard deviation

2   The required limit of accuracy or sampling error

3   The required level of confidence that the results will fall within a certain range.

Variance is a measure of how spread out a data set is. We work it out by looking at the average squared deviation of each number from its mean. There are different formulae for working out variance but the one most commonly used in market research takes into account the potential bias in a sample.

The formula is:
$$S^2 = \sum_{i=1}^{n} \frac{(X_i - \overline{X})^2}{n-1}$$

X is the individual value in an array of data

X overline {X} is the mean of the array

n is the number of values in an array

Σ = the Greek letter sigma, meaning 'sum of'

For example, for the set 1, 3, 6, 4 and 1, the number of values is 5, and the variance 4.5.

Value	Mean	Deviation	Deviation squared
1	3	−2	4
3	3	0	0
6	3	3	9
4	3	1	1
1	3	−2	4
Total			18

The variance is the sum of squared differences divided by the number of values minus 1; = 18/(5 − 1) = 4.5.

Standard deviation is the square root of the variance which we calculated above. It is used to compare the spread of data sets. The more spread a set of values, the higher the standard deviation. The formula is similar to that used to calculate variance.

$$SD = \sqrt{\frac{\Sigma(X_i - \overline{X})^2}{n-1}}$$

X_i = the value of each data point

X = the average of all the data points

Value	Mean	Deviation	Deviation squared
1	3	−2	4
3	3	0	0
6	3	3	9
4	3	1	1
1	3	−2	4
Total			18

The variance is the sum of squared differences divided by the number of values minus 1; = 18/(5 – 1) = 4.5.

The standard deviation is the square root of the variance or 2.12.

Normal distribution

Standard deviation is a measure of how widely values are dispersed from the average value (the mean). The higher the standard deviation, the more widely the values are spread. This allows us to use standard deviation to compare data sets.

In order to apply this to the determination of sample size, we need to understand another concept. That is normal distribution. This is an important concept. What it implies is that the distribution of values within any data set will be similar, for example shoe size, height or income, and will follow the pattern shown below – known as a bell-shaped curve.

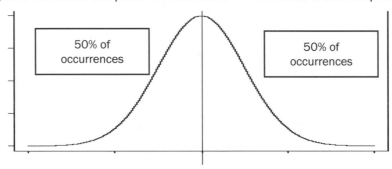

Figure 8.3: Normal distribution, the bell-shaped curve

So what does this mean? The area under the curve represents all occurrences. The line through the centre of the curve is the mean value.

Normal distribution has another key characteristic – 68 per cent of all occurrences fall within one standard deviation of the mean.

Normal distribution also tells us that 95 per cent of occurrences would fall between 1.96 standard deviations. This is very important as for the most part market researchers work at this level of certainty. What it means effectively is that there is a 1 in 20 chance of an occurrence falling outside this predicted range.

Normal distribution also tells us that 99 per cent of occurrences fall within 2.58 standard deviations.

The key point is that for any data set, the distribution of values is the same.

To repeat:

◆ 68 per cent of values fall within 1 standard deviation.

◆ 95 per cent fall within 1.96 standard deviations.

◆ 99 per cent fall within 2.58 standard deviations.

These percentages (68, 95 and 99 per cent) are known as confidence levels and are the same for all data sets that conform to a normal distribution. There are other types of distribution but you need not go further into this for the course.

For our purpose, marketers generally use 95 or 99 per cent confidence limits. These relate to 1.96 and 2.58 standard deviations and these are the confidence levels also known as Z values that are used. The upper and lower limit of the range that they indicate (for example = ±1.96) is called the confidence limit. The range itself is the confidence interval. Together these represent the most valuable tools for working out occurrences in the total market from a smaller sample.

There are two different ways of working out sample sizes for random samples, and these depend on whether we are measuring averages or proportions.

For studies involving averages or means

The formula to work out sample size is:

$$N = \frac{Z^2 \delta^2}{E^2}$$

Where, Z is the confidence level

δ is the population standard deviation

E is the acceptable level of precision.

Specify the level of precision

The level of precision is worked out by clients and researchers and reflects the budget available and the acceptable margin of error or degree of risk attached to the outcome of the research. If there is a need for accurate data, the sample size may be larger and the level of precision would be tighter.

Determine the acceptable confidence interval

As we have seen above, the standard level of confidence is 95 per cent. Remember, this means that at the 95 per cent confidence interval there is a 1 in 20 chance of the sample being wrong. If the level of risk was high, then we could work at the 99 per cent confidence level, here there is a 1 in a 100 chance of the sample being wrong.

Estimate the standard deviation

It is impossible to know this before carrying out the survey, so an estimate is required. This can be based upon:

◆ Previous studies

◆ Secondary research

◆ The result of pilot surveys

◆ Judgement.

Once the study is completed, the sample mean and standard deviation can be calculated, and the exact confidence level and limits of error can be worked out.

Remember the formula, and work through the example

$$N = \frac{Z^2 \delta^2}{E^2}$$

The sample required is 443.

Play around with the formula. Change the required level of precision and look at the impact on the sample size required.

Studies involving proportions

Studies measuring the proportion of a population having a certain characteristic are often required in marketing and in surveys, for example the proportion responding to a promotion or the number of voters against university top-up fees. To determine sample size here a different formula is needed.

Remember *Z* is our confidence level; let us use the standard marketing confidence level – so Z is 1.96 or the 95 per cent confidence level.

E is the limit of error. In this case we need the results to be correct to within let us say ±3 per cent, written as a decimal ±0.03.

P is the estimated percentage of the population who have the characteristic. In this case we will look at the number of people who may respond to a test mailing and we estimate that 15 per cent may respond. This again is written as a decimal –0.15.

So, let us work this through:

$$N = \frac{1.96 \times 1.96\,[0.15(1 - 0.15)]}{0.03^2}$$

We would therefore need a sample of 544 to be 95 per cent confident of our 15 per cent response rate on roll out of the campaign.

If we reduced the limits of error to ±1 per cent the sample size would increase.

$$N = \frac{0.4896}{0.0001}$$

$$N = 4896$$

If the estimated response was 2 per cent we can see the sample size would decrease.

$$N = \frac{3.84 \times 0.0196}{0.0001}$$

$$N = \frac{0.075}{0.0001}$$

$$N = 750$$

The figure reduces because the difference in the proportion of the population is higher.

If the estimated response rate went to 20 per cent, then the sample required would be 6144.

Adjustment for larger samples

We have said that there is no direct relationship between population and sample size to estimate a characteristic with a level of error and confidence.

The assumption is that sample elements are drawn independent of one another. This cannot be assumed when the sample is higher than 10 per cent of the population. If this is the case, an adjustment is made, called the finite population correction factor.

The calculation reduces the required sample:

$$N_1 = \frac{nN}{N + n - 1}$$

N_1 is the revised sample size

n is the original sample size

N is the population size.

For example, if the population has 2000 elements and the original sample size is 400:

$$N = \frac{400 \times 2000}{2000 + 400 - 1}$$

$$N = 333$$

Other rules-of-thumb factors to consider in setting sample sizes:

◆ Trade off cost against reliability and accuracy.

◆ Minimum subgroup sizes should be more than 100 respondents. It is difficult to be confident in figures lower than this.

◆ The average sample size in national surveys in the United Kingdom is around 1500–2000 respondents. Minimum sample sizes in the FMCG markets are 300–500 respondents.

Implementing a sampling procedure

Once the sample size is worked out, the researcher can start to gather data. We have already discussed the fact that a sample will always vary in some way from the population. There are a number of reasons for this.

Sampling error

'Sampling error is the error in a survey caused by using a sample to estimate the value of a parameter in the population' (ESOMAR, 2007).

'Sampling error is the difference between the sample value and the true value of a phenomenon for the population being surveyed' (Wilson, 2006).

Sampling error is inherent in the process of sampling and is reflected in the accuracy of estimates about the total population that can be made from the data. They can be estimated using statistics but other errors can occur. These are called non-sampling errors.

Non-sampling errors

◆ **Sampling frame error** – The error that occurs due to the fact that the sampling frame is different from the entire population. This can be reduced by combining lists to reinforce the frame.

◆ **Non-response error** – This may be due to refusal or the non-availability of respondents. Refusals can be reduced by incentivizing the process and through using trained, experienced interviewers and well-designed questionnaires.

◆ **Data error** – This may be through respondent error; responders give the wrong information deliberately or unintentionally. This can be reduced through careful analysis of inconsistency in the responses, through the use of well-designed questionnaires and the use of skilled interviewers.

◆ **Interviewer errors** – These occur as a result of the interviewer making mistakes in asking questions or recording answers. These can be reduced through careful training and back-checking to ensure that the interview was carried out, that the respondent matched the required profile, that all questions were asked and that the code of conduct of the MRS was adhered to. The IQCS ensure minimum standards for back-checking.

◆ **Data analysis error** – These can be caused by keystroke or software problems. They can be reduced by checking for consistency and manually profiling hard data against that held in the computer.

Weightings

Weightings are used to correct problems due to sampling error. Responses from subgroups are given a statistical weight reflecting the importance of the subgroup in the population of interest. The weighting is most often used to bring the sample into line with known proportions in the population, for example age or gender.

Panels

The use of panels is an important part of the marketing research industry and there are a range of panels covering everything from media consumption to business to business purchasing.

A panel is a form of survey from which comparative data is collected from the sampling units on more than one occasion. (Wilson 2006)

Information may be gathered by questionnaire, telephone interviews, diaries (documents where the respondent records their behaviour and purchases over a period such as a week or a month), barcode readers or through the Internet.

The key tasks involved in undertaking panel research are:

◆ The recruitment of a representative sample of the population that is willing and capable of doing the task.

◆ The maintenance of the members of the panel once recruited.

◆ Replacement of panel members who leave, with similar respondents so as to maintain consistency.

Panels may be used rather than one-off surveys to obtain dynamic information on:

◆ Broad trends in a market (e.g. are people moving from buying white bread to brown bread; which television programmes are more or less popular than previously).

◆ Case histories of specific respondents (e.g. level of repeat purchases, brand switching, reaction to special offers and advertising).

◆ Attitudes and reactions over time to particular products or services (a placement test is a type of panel where people's reactions to a new type of vacuum cleaner or car can be measured over time).

Summary

In this unit, we explored the process of sampling and looked in detail at the stages involved in the process:

◆   The definition of the population

◆   The decision to sample or census

◆   The creation of the sampling frame

◆   The sampling method.

We looked in detail at probability and non-probability sampling and the various approaches under each.

Probability sampling includes:

◆   Random sampling

◆   Systematic sampling

◆   Stratified random sampling

◆   Cluster sampling

◆   Area sampling.

Non-probability techniques include:

◆   Convenience sampling

◆   Judgement sampling

◆   Quota sampling

◆   Snowball sampling .

We looked at the constraints on the choice of sampling method.

The sample size was then discussed. Sample size is determined by financial, managerial and statistical considerations. We looked in detail at the statistical basis of establishing sample size.

We looked at the error involved in sampling and suggested ways of managing error and the process of weighting.

We explored the role of panels and the tasks involved in creating and maintaining them.

Bibliography

Crouch, S. and Housden, M. (2003) *Marketing Research for Managers*, Oxford: Elsevier Butterworth-Heinemann 3rd edition

Wilson, A. (2006) *Marketing Research: An Integrated Approach*, FT Prentice Hall, 2nd edition

Websites

ESOMAR (2007) www.esomar.org

MRS (2007) www.mrs.org.uk

Unit 9 Questionnaire design

Table 9.1: Learning outcomes and knowledge and skills requirements

Learning outcomes	Knowledge and skills requirements
4.6 Design a basic questionnaire and discussion guide to meet a project's research objectives	Design a basic questionnaire and discussion guide to meet a project's research objectives
	The questionnaire design process
	Question and response formats
	Scaling techniques (Likert and semantic differential)
	Sequence and wording
	Design layout and appearance
	Questionnaire generating software

Questionnaire – A structured data collection mechanism involving a range of question formats and completed orally or in print. Questionnaires may be administered by interviewers or self-completed by the respondent.

Coding – Turning responses into a form that enables analysis usually by allocating a unique number to each response.

Semantic differential – A scaling question that asks respondents to indicate the strength of their views on normally a 5- or 7-point scale between bipolar adjectives and statements.

Open questions – Questions that ask for the respondent's own response.

Dichotomous questions – Questions for which there are two possible replies.

Multiple choice questions – Questions with a number of predetermined answers.

Closed questions – Questions to which there are a limited number of predetermined responses.

Forced scale – A scaling question that does not allow for a neutral response.

Likert scales – A scaling approach that asks respondents to indicate their strength of agreement or disagreement with a range of statements on a 5-point scale.

Scaling questions – Questions assigning numerical values to subjective concepts.

Skip questions – Questions that take respondents to other questions determined by the answer.

Biased question – A question that is phrased so that it influences the answer.

Pilot study – A small-scale test of a completed questionnaire.

Study guide

This unit should take about two hours to complete.

Introduction

A questionnaire is a structured data-collection mechanism involving a range of question formats and completed orally or in print. This is distinct from a discussion guide or topic guide created for qualitative research in focus groups or depth interview that we looked at in detail in Unit 7.

The questionnaire is driven by the objectives of the research. It is important to design the questionnaire with this in mind. Often it is tempting to ask more questions than is strictly needed but respondents will not spend time completing a poorly constructed and unfocused questionnaire.

As we have seen, questionnaires may be administered by interviewers or self-completed by the respondent. The design of the questionnaire is a key task in the research and proves that good design can make the difference between a successful project and a failure.

The questionnaire has four main purposes. It is designed to:

(a) Collect relevant data

(b) Remove bias

(c) Make data comparable

(d) Motivate the respondent.

This unit will outline the process of developing a good questionnaire.

Figure 9.1: example of a PDA based survey.

Source: Reproduced with permission from www.snapsurveys.com

The questionnaire design process

Wilson (2006) identifies a process for questionnaire development:

1   Develop question topics

2   Select question and response formats

3   Determine sequence

4   Design layout and appearance

5   Pilot test

6   Undertake the survey.

Developing question topics

This process will draw on the results of any exploratory, desk or qualitative research carried out already. The research objectives laid down in the research brief and proposal will also be drawn on to inform the process. The idea is to make the questionnaire as efficient as possible. The questionnaire should produce the maximum amount of required information in minimum time.

The characteristics of the respondents should also be considered:

◆   Do they have the information we are asking for?

◆   Will they be able to remember the information?

◆   Are they likely to tell us the information we are asking for? Is it particularly sensitive data, for example income, sexual practices and so on?

◆   How literate and numerate are they? Will they be able to articulate the information?

◆   Will they understand the questions?

◆   Will they be interested in the survey?

Question and response formats

What does a questionnaire contain?

There are three parts to any questionnaire:

1   Identification data

2   Classification data

3   Subject data.

Identification data – It is usually completed by the interviewer. It contains identification of the respondent, maybe name, address and a contact number.

It will also include the time, date and place of the interview and name of the interviewer, and sometimes a unique number to identify the questionnaire itself.

This data is required to allow checkbacks to be made. It is important to note that the MRS code of conduct aims to ensure the anonymity of the respondent.

Classification data – It is the data that is required to classify respondents. It may include

◆   Age

◆   Gender

◆   Income

◆   Job title

◆   Marital status.

This allows the information to be analysed effectively and also to help the interviewer ensure that the respondent has the characteristics of the sample that is required to be interviewed.

Both identification and classification questions may be kept to the end of the question-naire to allow sufficient rapport to be built-up between the interviewer and the respondent, unless they are needed to establish quotas.

Subject data – It refers to the nature of the information that is being gathered to meet the survey objectives. This may be laid down in a flow diagram which allows us to begin to plan the question sequence.

This flow chart is a route map through the questionnaire to be created in outline and allows the designer to introduce what are known as 'skip' or 'filter' questions to take the respondent through the questionnaire.

For example:

Do you drink wine?

>   If YES go to Q.2

>   If NO go to Q.9

Care needs to be taken in the use of skip questions; too many can be confusing to a respondent who is self-completing or to an inexperienced interviewer. The use of CATI and CAPI systems can help here as the computer will go to the appropriate question automatically, given the response to the skip question.

Cushion statements help with the flow and management of the questionnaire, e.g.:

That complete the first part of the questionnaire I am now going to ask you some questions about the store.

Cushion statements and skip and routing questions are often printed in a different colour to distinguish them from the questionnaire itself.

What type of questions can be asked?

There are four main question types. These are:

1   Closed questions

      (a) Dichotomous

      (b) Multiple choice

2   Open-ended

3   Rating scales.

Closed questions – dichotomous

Simply these are questions to which there are only two possible answers, for example 'yes' and 'no'. This sounds simple but the question asked must fit into this answer structure. A question that asks:

'Do you intend to go on holiday in the next 12 months?' may be answered:

'It depends'.

For completeness a 'don't know' option is usually offered. For example:

1. Do you bank online?

	Code
Yes	1
No	2
Don't know	3

Each of these is given a code number for analysis. In the example above the code is 11 (i.e. question 1, answer code 1), if the respondent had answered 'No' the code would be 12.

Closed questions – multiple choice

These appear straightforward but are quite difficult to construct as the designer needs to know all possible answers. This is known as being 'collectively exhaustive'. This can be achieved by piloting the questionnaire to ensure that all possible answers are offered.

To avoid this, the 'other' response is often used and this usually leaves a space to allow the response to be written onto the questionnaire. Other answers are coded later to produce a full list of codes for analysis (a coding frame).

'How do you usually travel to work?'

	Code
Car	1
Train	2
Bus	3
Bicycle	4
Walk	5
Motorbike or scooter	6
Other..	

It is important that when multiple choice questions are being designed the answers are mutually exclusive. This means that there is no overlap between responses. This is important in dealing with details of age or quantities and is easy to miss.

A major petrol retailer produced a questionnaire with the following question:

'On average what mileage do you get each year?'

0–5000

5000–10,000

10,000–15,000

15,000–20,000

More than 20,000

Spot the problem? Yes, there is overlap. The responses are not mutually exclusive. Red faces all round!

Other issues with multiple choice responses include the number of potential responses. This may mean that the respondent cannot remember the first answers. In face-to-face interviews the responses may be put on a show card (Figure 9.2). This is not always possible in other media.

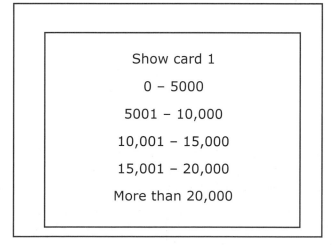

Show card 1

0 – 5000

5001 – 10,000

10,001 – 15,000

15,001 – 20,000

More than 20,000

Figure 9.2: Show cards

Open-ended questions

Open-ended questions are questions in which an answer is not suggested. The respondent is free to respond in any way. Because of this, they are sometimes known as unstructured questions. It may be that a one-word answer is required or it may be that a longer response is needed. For example:

◆ Why did you choose to study with the CIM?

◆ What do you enjoy most about your course?

◆ What would you like to change about the course?

The problem with open questions is analysis. If there are very many categories of answers, then it may be hard to code the responses and it may reduce the effectiveness of the analysis.

Much depends on the skill of the researcher in these cases.

One way around this is to pilot the survey and produce a pre-coded list of potential responses which allows the interviewer to interpret the response and code it.

Open-ended questions can be very useful and the difficulties in managing them within a questionnaire are not huge. Their value can certainly outweigh these difficulties.

Scaling questions

There are many types of scaling questions. They are very useful in quantifying complex and multi-dimensional concepts such as opinions, attitudes and motivation. A scale question will ask a respondent to indicate the strength of feeling about that concept. This may be done on a multidimensional basis, for example exploring the range of different aspects of a brand or company, or it may be done on a single dimension, for example the satisfaction with that brand or company. The quantification allows comparison to be made.

Graphic versus itemized scales

Scales can be itemized or graphic.

A graphical scale asks the respondent to indicate the level they associate with the issue on a line.

Dissatisfied_____X_____Satisfied

Occasionally a value may be added whilst still allowing free selection.

Dissatisfied_____ 1_____2_____3_____4_____5___X___6_____Satisfied

Itemized scales are easier to complete and to analyse. The graphical responses are translate into clear vales.

Indicate your opinion about CIM courses

CIM courses are poor value   1   2   3   4   5   CIM courses are good value

Comparative versus non-comparative assessments

Wilson (2006) defines comparative rating scales as scales that ask respondents to compare the organization or issues in relation to a common frame of reference. Non-comparative allows the respondents to select their own frame of reference.

The comparative approach can be used to allow companies to rate their performance relative to others, or in evaluating the features that a consumer values in a product.

An example from industry can be seen in train companies asking customers to rank speed of journey, the price of the journey, on-board facilities and station facilities.

Forced versus non-forced scales

Forced scales do not allow a neutral position. For example:

A forced scale:

Do you think that CIM courses are:

| Very inexpensive | Inexpensive | Expensive | Very expensive |

An unforced scale:

Do you think that CIM courses are

| Very inexpensive | Inexpensive | Neither inexpensive nor expensive | Expensive | Very expensive |

Forced scales can be used when it is believed that there will be few neutral respondents. These are used also to force those who are in the neutral position to decide and can lead to spurious data being obtained.

Balanced versus unbalanced scales

Balanced scales have a balanced number of positive and negative responses. Unbalanced may be used when piloting has suggested that there will be fewer of a particular response and also to explore the more common position with more sensitivity.

Number of scale positions

There are no hard and fast rules as to the number of positions on a scale. The most common number is 5. Some researchers use 7 or 9. The idea is that there is greater sensitivity in using a higher number. The key consideration is that respondents are able to make a clear distinction between the various options.

Labelling and pictorial representation of positions

Scales generally require at least two 'anchor' labels at each end of the scale. As we have seen earlier, it is also possible to label each position.

It is also possible to use emoticons (Figure 9.3); smiley faces or thumbs up or down can be useful in certain markets and may be useful in international markets but you need to be careful with thumbs up which has a very rude meaning in some markets.

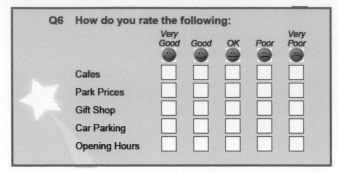

Figure 9.3: The use of emoticons in scale questions.

Source: Reproduced with permission from www.snapsurveys.com

Commonly used scales

Respondents divide certain points or other units (possibly currency) between a number of attributes.

This gives a rank order of attributes and an indication of the scale of difference between these attributes.

Train companies have used this type of research, allocating consumers a number of pounds and giving them a range of investment opportunities on which to spend them.

Likert scales

A commonly used scale, the Likert scale asks respondents to indicate their level of agreement with a range of statements. Responses are scored from 1 to 5 and the result is an average score for each statement indicating the level of agreement with the statement, where 1 is strongly disagree and 5 is strongly agree.

	Strongly disagree				Strongly agree
CIM courses are good value	1	2	3	4	5
CIM courses are relevant to my needs	1	2	3	4	5
My CIM course is enjoyable	1	2	3	4	5

Figure 9.4: A Likert scale

The strength of the Likert scale depends on the way that the statements are selected. This involves filtering and pre-testing a range of statements before the final statements are selected. The initial list may be generated as a result of qualitative or exploratory research.

Activity 9.1

Create a list of 20 statements for a Likert scale about a product of your choice.

Test this list on a friend or colleague. How effective was your list? What have you learned from the test?

Semantic differentials

Semantic differentials use words or statements and their opposites and measure the strength of opinion between them (Figure 9.5).

The words are generated from exploratory or qualitative research, and may be used for example, to rate a single brand or to compare brands.

	1	2	3	4	5	
Expensive	◆	■ 2	3	4	5	Inexpensive
Effective	◆ 1	2	3	■ 4	5	Ineffective
For career women	1	◆ 2	3	■ 4	5	For the housewife
Modern	◆ 1	2	3	■ 4	5	Old-fashioned

Key:

Brand A ◆

Brand B ■

Figure 9.5: Semantic differentials

Purchase intent scales

These scales are used to measure the respondents' intention to buy a product or a potential product.

They look like the following example:

If this car was priced at £5,999, would you:

Definitely buy	1
Probably buy	2
Probably not buy	3
Definitely not buy	4

Select wording and phrasing

The next stage of the questionnaire is to word the questions. At each stage of the process, the researcher should stop and ask 'Is the question really necessary?' Each question should be carefully evaluated on its own, in relation to other questions on the questionnaire and the overall objectives of the study. If the question does not contribute to the overall purpose of the research, it should not be included in the questionnaire.

There are many rules on questionnaire wording:

Ensure meaning is understood. For example, is dinner a meal consumed at night or at 'lunch' time. In international markets this is more important. Translation of questionnaires can cause major problems. The secret is to translate and then back translate into the original language.

A question that was asked to young people, 'What was the prime motivator behind your impulse purchase of confectionery countlines?' is clearly inappropriate for the audience. The language of the audience is important and this is one of the functions of qualitative research to allow the questionnaire to be constructed using appropriate terms.

Insight: Sexual health and the researcher

HIV has meant that an understanding of the sexual behaviour of the population is important for health budgeting and provision. Market research has been used to find out this very sensitive and important information.

A questionnaire was designed to present a range of behaviours in language that all respondents could understand.

Qualitative research via focus groups informed the language of the questionnaire. Whilst the terms cannot be repeated here, it meant that the quantitative phase of the study was far more successful.

Other rules on questionnaire wording

Use clear and simple language. Use words of one or two syllables. Use simple English:

◆ Instead of 'observe', use 'look'

◆ Instead of 'construct', use 'build'

◆ Instead of 'regarding', use 'about'

◆ Instead of 'at this moment in time', use 'now'.

Use what is known as demotic language or the language of the people. It is very easy to produce stiff and inaccessible written words. Remember, very often the questionnaire will be read out loud. It is good practice to speak the question.

◆ Avoid ambiguity:
'Do you buy a newspaper regularly?'
What does regular mean? Every day? O nce a month? Once a year?

◆ Avoid two questions in one:
'What do you think of our prices and product quality?'
It is impossible to answer this accurately.

◆ Avoid leading or loaded questions:
'Should the council spend money regenerating the poor environment in Brookmill ward?'
It is hard for anyone to disagree with this question. 'Most people think that our membership of the European Union is a good thing, Do you?' is a classic leading question. The aim has to be to reduce the potential to lead respondents.

◆ Avoid assumptions:
'When driving, do you listen to your CD player?'
This makes a number of assumptions about respondents: that they drive, that their cars have CD players, even that they are not hearing impaired!!

◆ Avoid generalization:

'How much do you usually spend on beer in a week?'
There are much better observational or panel methodologies to ensure accuracy here. If the respondent is spending more than a few pounds, the chances are that he will not remember in any case!

◆ Avoid negative questions:

'You don't think that drink-driving should be more strictly regulated, do you?'
is confusing and leads to problems.

◆ Avoid hypothetical questions:

'If West Ham were relegated, would you still buy a season ticket?'
Speculation and guesswork is an outcome of this type of question.

Activity 9.2

Using the rules above try to work out what is wrong with the following questions:
* Are you single?
* What is your average weekly disposable income?
* How regularly do you come here?
* Do you buy green vegetables?
* Do you by frozen and canned foods?
* What about our chilled and ambient ready meals?
* How much did you spend on food last year?
* Most people say our new store layout is really good. What do you think?
* Does your husband come with you?
* When do you leave the car?
* Are you against drug abuse?
* You don't think council tax is too high, do you?
* If we moved to the high street would you come more often?
* How old are your children?

       0–3
       3–5
       5–10
       10–15
       15+

A better approach

This is an extract from a questionnaire evaluating a newsagent.

* What is your postcode? ....

* How did you get from home to this store?

Car	O
Motorcycle	O
Bus	O
Train	O
Foot	O
Cycle	O
Other	

    Please state: ....

Did you buy any of the following today (SHOW CARD):

Newspapers and magazines	O
Sandwiches	O
Other snacks	O
Drinks	O
Confectionery	O
Other	

    Please state ....

On a scale of 1–5, how would you rate the following aspects of this store, where 1 is very poor and 5 is very good.

	1	2	3	4	5
Cleanliness of the store	O	O	O	O	O
Product selection	O	O	O	O	O
Helpfulness of staff	O	O	O	O	O
Speed through the checkout	O	O	O	O	O

Thank you for your help.

Sequencing

Wilson suggests that the questionnaires should be funnel-sequenced, that is going from the broad to the narrow. The interviewer asks the most general questions about the subject and moves to narrower and more focused questions. For example:

◆   How do you rate the quality of management education in the United Kingdom?

◆   How do you rate the quality of business education in the marketing research sector?

◆   How do you rate the MRS diploma?

It is useful to start the questionnaire with some fairly straightforward questions to get the interview going. Questions about identity, occupation, family and marital status, and educational level might be included here.

Classification questions may have to be asked early to ensure that the respondent fits the intended responder profile.

Algood Moving in Survey 2007

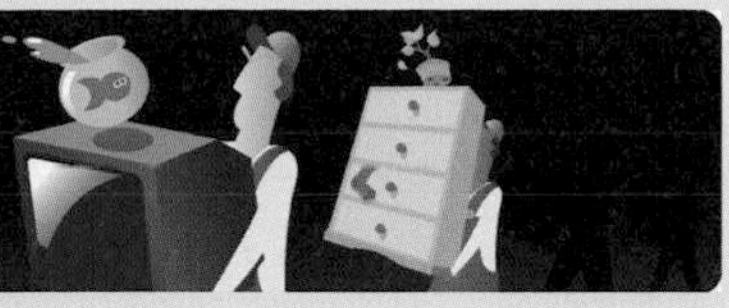

Please tick the boxes that most closely match your personal opinions

Q1 How would you rate your current accommodation?

Very Good......... ☐ *Good*................ ☐ *Acceptable*........ ☐ *Poor*................. ☐ *Very Poor*.......... ☐

Q2 Please indicate how important you rate the following factors of your current property?

	Very Important	*Important*	*Neither Important nor Unimportant*	*Not Important*	*Unimportant*
Size of individual plots	☐	☐	☐	☐	☐
Access to train station	☐	☐	☐	☐	☐
Layout of estate	☐	☐	☐	☐	☐
Open space	☐	☐	☐	☐	☐
Local Schools	☐	☐	☐	☐	☐

Q3 Please indicate how satisified you are with the following factors of your current property?

	Very satisfied	*Satisfied*	*Neither satisfied nor dissatisfied*	*Dissatisfied*	*Very Dissatisfied*
Size of individual plots	☐	☐	☐	☐	☐
Access to train station	☐	☐	☐	☐	☐
Layout of estate	☐	☐	☐	☐	☐
Open space	☐	☐	☐	☐	☐
Local schools	☐	☐	☐	☐	☐

Q4 Why do you want to move (please do not tick more than 3)?

- *House too small*........ ☐
- *House too large*........ ☐
- *Want a garden*........ ☐
- *Problems with neighbours*........ ☐
- *Dislike this area*........ ☐
- *Medical reasons*........ ☐
- *Too far from job*........ ☐
- *None of the above*........ ☐

Q5 Do you want to move to:

- *Another council property*........ ☐
- *Privately rented property*........ ☐
- *Owner occupied property*........ ☐
- *Housing association property*........ ☐
- *Other*........ ☐

Q6 Do you have any dependants?

Yes ...... ☐ *No*........ ☐ Go to Q8

Q7 If you answered yes,how many children under 16 live in your household ?

☐

Q8 Are you male or female?

- *Male*........ ☐
- *Female*........ ☐

Q9 What is your age?

- *Under 18*........ ☐
- *18 to 24*........ ☐
- *25 to 44*........ ☐
- *45 to 60*........ ☐
- *Over 60*........ ☐

Q10 Do you have internet access?

- *Yes*........ ☐
- *No*........ ☐

Q11 What is your email address?

☐

Thank you for taking the time to complete this form.

Figure 9.6: An example of a short paper-based survey.

Source: Reproduced with permission from www. Snapsurveys.com

This questionnaire about marketing includes classification questions as the first section:

Section 1: We need to know a few things about you:

1   Title: Mr/Mrs/Ms/Miss/Dr/Professor/Other (please state): _____

2   First name: _____

3   Last name: _____

4   Job title:_____

5   Company: _____

6   Number of employees working in your company: _____

7   Number of employees working in marketing:_____

8   What are your key areas of responsibility (please tick all those that apply)?

☐ Public relations	☐ Planning	☐ Intranet
☐ Advertising	☐ Internet	☐ Events
☐ Exhibitions	☐ Research	
☐ Sales force management	☐ Brand management	
☐ Database management	☐ E-commerce	
☐ Product management	☐ Data analysis	
☐ Campaign management	☐ Call centre management	
☐ Media buying	☐ Sales promotion	
☐ Other (please state):_____		

9   Which of the following marketing publications do you read?

	Every week	From time to time
Marketing	☐	☐
Marketing Week	☐	☐
Admap	☐	☐
Campaign	☐	☐
Creative Review	☐	☐
Precision Marketing	☐	☐
Direct Marketing Week	☐	☐
Revolution	☐	☐
New Media Age	☐	☐
DM Business	☐	☐
Media Week	☐	☐
Customer Relationship	☐	☐
Management	☐	☐
Marketing Direct	☐	☐
Direct response	☐	☐
Other	☐	☐
Please give title(s):_____		

Other sensitive questions, for example on age or income, might be better left to the end of the questionnaire to ensure that a rapport has been established.

Design, layout and appearance

The physical appearance of the questionnaire will determine levels of response even if the questionnaire is interview-administered.

◆ It needs to be spaced effectively, not squashed onto one page – that may save money but will reduce response.

◆ If it is to be used outside, a book format might protect the questionnaire better.

◆ It needs to be set in at least 10-point type so that people can read the wording.

◆ It needs to be produced to a high quality with no literals and printed on high-quality paper.

◆ It should look interesting. Colour can help.

◆ A range of question types can help make the questionnaire more engaging.

◆ Coding and interviewer instructions must be clearly distinguished from the questions.

◆ Use skip and filter questions and routing instructions to help the interviewer or respondent work through the questionnaire.

Insight: Computer software and questionnaire design

There are a range of packages on the market that will help with the process of questionnaire design. Snap is one of the best (www.snapsurveys.com).

Software such as Snap will allow you to design and deliver a survey in a variety of formats including online or paper-based and will also allow the creation of sophisticated analysis and related tables. Data can also be exported to other software for further analysis in Excel or SPSS for example.

Pilot

Piloting or testing the questionnaire is crucial. It:

◆ Allows problems to be corrected

◆ Helps with the coding process

◆ Improves question sequencing

◆ Improves wording of questions.

Piloting can be done with a small sample but it must be done. If many changes are made, the revised questionnaire should also be piloted. Piloting should be carried out by the staff who will administer the questionnaire, in a comparable environment and with respondents who share the characteristics of the sample.

◆ The **debriefing** method means the respondents should be asked afterwards what their thought processes were as they completed the questionnaire.

◆ The **protocol** method allows the respondent to talk through the process of completing the questionnaire.

Questionnaire checklist

◆ Are the objectives right?

◆ Will the data specified meet the objectives?

◆ Will the questions listed collect all the data required?

◆ Is every question essential?

◆ Will the right type of data be collected for:
 ◆ Fact?
 ◆ Opinion?
 ◆ Motive?

◆ Will all the identification data required be collected?

◆ Will all the classification data required be collected?

◆ Is the question sequence logical?

◆ Are the types of question being used appropriate:
 ◆ Dichotomous?
 ◆ Multiple-choice?
 ◆ Open-ended?
 ◆ Rating scales?

◆ Is the question wording:
 ◆ Simple to understand?
 ◆ Unambiguous?
 ◆ Clear?

◆ Have cushion statements been used when necessary?

◆ Is it reasonable to expect the respondent to answer every question?

◆ Will the answers be easy to record?

◆ Will the answers be easy to process?

◆ Does the questionnaire look good?

◆ Will it, and any show material, be easy for the interviewers to use?

◆ Has the questionnaire been piloted?

◆ Is the right type of questionnaire being used:
 ◆ Personal?
 ◆ Postal?
 ◆ Telephone?
 ◆ Online?

Source: Crouch and Housden (2003)

Summary

In this unit we looked at the process of designing a questionnaire.

The questionnaire has four main purposes. It is designed to:

◆ Collect relevant data

◆ Remove bias

◆ Make data comparable

◆ Motivate the respondent.

We looked at a process for questionnaire development:

◆ Develop question topics

◆ Select question and response formats

◆ Determine sequence

◆ Design layout and appearance

◆ Pilot test

◆ Undertake the survey.

We looked at the process of developing question topics.

We explored in depth the types of questions that can be asked which included:

◆ Closed dichotomous questions

◆ Closed multiple-choice questions

◆ Open questions

◆ Scale questions, including:

  ◆ Likert scales

  ◆ Semantic differential

  ◆ Intention to buy scales

  ◆ Forced and unforced scales.

We explored the wording of questions and their sequencing. We saw that there were a number of rules of right wording and phrasing of questionnaires.

◆ Use clear and simple language

◆ Avoid ambiguity

◆ Avoid two questions in one

◆ Avoid leading or loaded questions

◆ Avoid assumptions

◆ Avoid generalization

◆ Avoid negative questions

◆ Avoid hypothetical questions.

We looked at the design and appearance of the completed questionnaire and the various ways of improving this aspect of questionnaire design. We saw that:

◆ It should be laid out effectively in a clear font.

◆ It should be set in a practical format.

◆ It should be produced to a high quality with no literals and printed on high-quality paper.

◆ It should look interesting with a range of question types.

◆ Coding and interviewer instructions must be clearly distinguished from the questions.

Finally, we looked at the importance of the pilot, a small-scale test of the completed questionnaire and a checklist was provided to help judge the quality of the questionnaire.

Bibliography

Crouch, S.and Housden, M. (2003) *Marketing Research for Managers*, Oxford: Elsevier Butterworth-Heinemann, 3rd edition

Wilson, A. (2006) *Marketing Research: An Integrated Approach*, FT Prentice Hall, 2nd edition

Websites

CIM 2007 www.cim.co.uk

www.snapsurveys.com

Unit 10

Quantitative analysis and the presentation of results

Learning objectives

After completing this unit you will be able to:

◆ Understand the process of data management, entry, editing, coding and cleaning.

◆ Understand concepts of tabulation and statistical analysis.

◆ Understand the use of computer packages that can help with the process.

◆ Understand the audience/audience thinking sequence.

◆ Understand the physical and on-line research report format.

◆ Understand the oral presentation format.

◆ Use tables and graphs.

Table 10.1: Learning outcomes and knowledge and skills requirements

Learning outcomes	Knowledge and skills requirements
1.4 Review the key elements and formats when reporting or presenting marketing information to decision-makers	Understanding the audience/audience thinking sequence
	Physical and online research report format
	Oral presentation format
	Using tables and graphs
	Understand the analysis phase of the marketing research process

Key definitions

Coding – The process that allocates a number to each answer and it is this that allows analysis to take place.

Editing – The process of computer or manual checking of the data to look for respondent or interview errors.

Frequency distributions – Counts of the numbers of respondents who gave each possible answer to a particular question.

Nominal data – Numbers assigned to objects or phenomena as labels or identification numbers that name or classify but that have no true numeric meaning (Wilson, 2006).

Ordinal data – Numbers with the labelling characteristics of nominal data but which also have the ability to communicate the rank order of the data. They do not indicate absolute quantities and do not imply that the intervals between the numbers are equal (Wilson, 2006).

Interval data – Similar to ordinal data but with the added dimension that intervals between the values on a scale are equal (Wilson, 2006).

Ratio data – Actual or real numbers that have a meaningful or absolute zero (Wilson, 2006).

Descriptive statistics – Statistical devices that help to summarize data. These include measures of central tendency, mode, mean, median and measures of dispersion range, inter-quartile range and standard deviation.

Factor analysis – Studies the relationships between variables to simplify data into a smaller set of composite variables or factors.

Correlation – Examines the strength of the relationship between variables using an index.

Cross tabulations – Table setting out responses to one question relative to others.

Coefficient of determination – Measure of the strength of linear relationship between a dependent and an independent variable.

Conjoint analysis – Analysis that asks respondents to make decisions between various attributes measuring their relative importance.

Chi square – A test measuring the goodness of fit between the observed sample values and the expected distribution of those values.

Z test – A hypothesis test about a single mean where the sample is greater than 30.

T Test – A hypothesis test about a single mean where the sample is less than 30.

Spearman's rank order correlation – Correlation for ordinal data.

Pearson's product moment correlation – A correlation technique for interval and ratio data.

Oral presentation – A verbal presentation of research findings using a range of supporting material.

Executive summary – A precis of the report.

Study guide

The unit should take around two hours to complete.

introduction

The analysis of data is a key skill of the marketing manager. Very often people find the introduction of statistics a little daunting. However, an ability to understand basic methods of data analysis is very important. This unit will take you through the process of preparing data and analysing that data to inform marketing decisions. For the less numerate, it will try to show you what the various techniques do to data, and how and why they are used. Many people find that describing what the techniques do in words makes the whole task more manageable and accessible.

Data analysis can be done easily now using computer packages such as Excel and SPSS. However, the lack of understanding of the techniques remains. The statistical packages are of no use at all unless you understand what you are trying to do to the data and which technique is most appropriate. You also need to be able to interpret the results. This is what we will try to do here. If you are taking the continuous assessment route through the course, then this area will be important to help you present research data effectively.

Editing and coding

Before data is processed, it is assessed for completeness and coherence. The editing process involves computer or manual checking of the data to look for respondent or interview errors or inconsistencies. If errors are identified, the respondent may be called back and if the questionnaire cannot be rescued, then it may be rejected.

Coding is the process that allocates a number to each answer and it is this that allows analysis to take place. As discussed earlier, the coding process may take place as the questionnaire is administered either manually by the interviewer ringing a number on the questionnaire or it may be managed through computer-assisted methods.

After this process is completed the data will look like this:

	Question 1	Question 2	Question 3	Question 4	Etc.
Record 1	1	3	1	10	
Record 2	1	4	5	15	
Record 3	2	2	3	12	
Etc...					

The questionnaire might have looked like this:

Question 1	Code
Sex	
M	1
F	2

Question 2	Code
What is your age?	
18–25	1
26–35	2
36–45	3
46–55	4
55+	5

And so on.

Coding open questions involves using a sample of the completed questionnaires and developing a coding frame or a list of codes for all possible responses to the questions. This may categorize and group certain diverse responses into a manageable number. This process must be handled carefully to reduce the processing error that might occur. The key thing is to learn from the piloting of the questionnaire and to analyse all possible responses. However, in certain questions the number of coded responses may need to be limited to ensure efficient operation of the survey; in this case, the coder or interviewer needs to be confident in allocating a certain response to a broader coded category (Figure 10.1).

Question 1	
What did you enjoy during the purchase of your car?	
Salespeople	1
Dealership facilities	2
Test drive	3
Negotiations over price	4
Follow-up calls	5
Information pack	6
Other code	7

Figure 10.1: Example of a coding frame for an open question

Data entry

Data entry may be carried out automatically through CAPI, CAWI and CATI systems or entries scanned into the computer using optical character recognition software or entered by hand. After this process, the data will be once again checked or cleaned for keystroke or character recognition problems. Once this is done, the data can be analysed.

Tabulation and statistical analysis

There are four types of data that can be analysed. These are:

(a) Nominal data

(b) Ordinal data

(c) Interval data

(d) Ratio data.

Nominal data

These refer to values that are given to objects that in themselves have no intrinsic numerical value. For example, we assigned a value to gender: 1 for men and 2 for women. We can count them and create percentages.

Statistics based on frequency counts can be used with this type of data. These include mode, that is, most frequently occurring value and chi-square tests, that is, a test that shows whether or not the results taken from a small sample are statistically significant from the expected results in the population as a whole.

The mode is the most frequently occurring figure in a set of data. For example, this may be used to say that Brand X was the most frequently mentioned brand.

Chi square tests measure the significance between cross-tabulated data. For example, we may have data that shows that men buy more beer than women. Whilst we might assume that this is the case, we will have a range of values in each cell. The problem is to determine if the difference in the values is real or a result of using a sample of the population, rather than asking the whole population.

If you are struggling with these concepts, do not worry; we will explore them in more detail later in this unit.

Ordinal data

This data represents rank order. It does not imply that there is an equal gap between items ranked and there is no other meaning to them other than rank order.

Examples include asking consumers to rank a number of products 1–5 around a certain attribute. For example:

Rank the following online banks 1–5 in order of their reputation for service where 1 is the bank which offers the best service and 5 is the bank that offers the worst service.

◆ Smile
◆ Cahoot
◆ First Direct
◆ Egg
◆ Intelligent Finance.

We can use mode and median analysis with this data.

The median is the middle value when responses are arranged in order.

Interval data

It is rank order data in which the intervals between the data are equal. These are also known as interval scales. Interval scales rank elements relative to each other but not from any observable origin. This means that the data has its meaning only by virtue of the comparison between elements selected. This means that ratio analysis between values is not possible.

Rank the following online banks 1–5 in order of their reputation for service, where 1 is the bank which offers the best service and 5 is the bank that offers worst service.

Smile	1	2	3	4	5
Cahoot	1	2	3	4	5
First Direct	1	2	3	4	5
Egg	1	2	3	4	5
Intelligent Finance	1	2	3	4	5

This data allows means and standard deviations to take place and a range of other statistical tests can be carried out.

The mean is the average of the results.

Standard deviation is a measure that looks at the distribution of results around the average value of the results.

Ratio data

Ratio data has an absolute zero or observable origin, for example shoe size, products bought or age.

This means all analyses are possible.

Tabulations, hole counts and frequency

Tables give researchers a feel for data. Frequency distributions are simply counts of the numbers of respondents who gave each possible answer to a particular question. They are used to help the researcher form the next stage of analysis.

Cross-tabulations (cross-tabs)

These tables 'cross' the answers to one question with the answers to another, for example age of respondent and products purchased (Figure 10.2).

Q. 15 When do you plan to buy a new car?

Base: All those who intend to replace their car

	Total	Age	
		21–44	**45+**
Base	127 (100%)	67 (100%)	60 (100%)
Within a month	12 (9%)	2 (3%)	10 (17%)
Within 6 months	45 (35%)	25 (37%)	20 (33%)
Within the year	55 (43%)	30 (45%)	25 (42%)
Longer	15 (12%)	10 (15%)	5 (8%)

Tables can be presented graphically.

It is easy to generate cross-tabs using computers. The skill is to decide which analyses are relevant and significant.

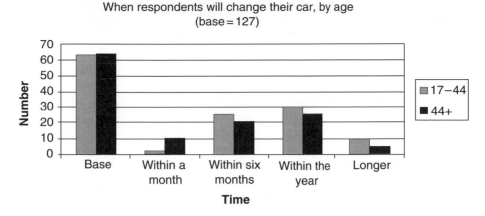

Figure 10.2: Cross-tabulations

Descriptive statistics

These are used to give the researcher a view of the location of the data and its spread. They are known as measures of central tendency and measures of dispersion or variability.

Measures of central tendency indicate typical values for data sets. These are the mean, median and mode.

The mean is the arithmetic average. To calculate the mean, divide the total values by the number of cases.

The median is the value of the middle case in a series of numbers put in ascending or descending order.

The mode is the value in a set of data that appears most frequently. A data set may have more than one mode – several categories may be equal and share the highest frequency.

For example, shoe sizes bought in one hour:

5	6	6	7	8
9	8	8	8	8
9	9	9	8	8
11	10	10	9	9
11	12	12	13	5

Mode = 8   Median = 9   Mean = 8.72

Measures of dispersion

These indicate how spread out or dispersed a data set is. We looked at these in Unit 8 and you should revisit this unit as required. Remember they include the range, variance and standard deviation.

The range is the interval from the highest to the lowest value in a data set. In the example above, the range is 13–5 = 8.

The shoe example is straightforward. However, if the size 13 man had bought 5 pairs of shoes, then the sample would be skewed towards the higher range. This is managed by using what is called the inter-quartile range; this removes any values that fall outside the 75th and 25th percentile and then calculates the range.

Remember, variance is a measure of how spread out a data set is, and we work it out by looking at the average squared deviation of each number from its mean.

Let us look at the formula once again.

$$S^2 = \sum_{i=1}^{n} \frac{(X_i - \overline{X})^2}{n - 1}$$

X is the individual value in an array of data

$\overline{X}$ is the mean of the array

n is the number of values in an array.

Standard deviation is the square root of the variance. Look once again at the formula:

$$SD = \sqrt{\frac{\sum(X_i - \overline{X})^2}{n - 1}}$$

where

X_i = the value of each data point

$\overline{X}$ = the average of all the data points

Σ = the Greek letter sigma, meaning 'sum of'

n = the total number of data points.

Statistical significance

There are advantages to using samples rather than collecting data from the whole population under review. However, the data from a sample will always be subject to error. We cannot be sure that the difference between two results is a real change in those values or simply a result of the sampling error.

Clearly, there may be a mathematical difference between two values but if the difference is large enough not to have occurred through chance or error, then the difference is defined as statistically significant.

Hypothesis testing

A hypothesis is defined by Wilson as an assumption about a characteristic in the population. Research will allow the researcher to conclude something about the population.

For example, in a survey of 500 customers the average number of times a customer purchased from a store was found to be approximately 4 times per month or 50 times per year. Managers believed the actual frequency to be 60 times. Is the sample consistent with our marketing managers' beliefs? The sample has a standard deviation of 10.

The testing of hypothesis follows a simple structure. First, establish the hypothesis.

There are two forms of hypotheses:

1   The null hypothesis or H0 is the one that will be tested, that is, the existing situation where no difference is expected.

2   The alternative hypothesis or H1 is the one in which a difference is expected.

For example, our recall problem could be expressed as:

The null hypothesis or H0, mean purchase frequency is 60 times per year.

The alternative hypothesis or H1, mean purchase frequency is not 60 times per year.

If we use the 95 per cent confidence level we can work this out.

Standard error is

$$\frac{10}{\sqrt{500}} = 0.45$$

The sample mean is 8 lower than the hypothesized mean 8/0.45 = 17.88 standard errors below the mean.

At 95 per cent confidence we would expect the sample mean to be within 1.96 standard errors of our null hypothesis. Because it is not, we cannot reject the null hypothesis.

The hypotheses will either be accepted or rejected depending on the outcome of the results.

There are a range of significance tests available and the most frequently used tests are:

◆   Chi-square test

◆   Z test

◆   T Test.

Significance tests measure whether the difference between two percentages is significant or not, or whether the difference between two means from different samples is significant. In order to carry out these tests three concepts must be considered.

Degrees of freedom

Degrees of freedom are defined as the number of observations minus 1. A sample n has $n-1$ degrees of freedom. Degrees of freedom are used to reflect potential bias in a sample.

Independent versus related samples

Selection of the appropriate test technique may involve considering whether samples are independent or related. In related samples, the measurement of the variable of interest in one sample might affect the measurement of the variable of interest in another.

Errors in hypothesis testing

Two types of error are known – type one and type two. A concept called the alpha level defines the probability of committing such an error and is commonly set at 0.05 or a 5 per cent chance of the error occurring.

Type one errors happen when the null hypothesis is rejected when it is true. Type two errors mean accepting the null hypothesis when it is false.

Reducing the alpha level increases the chance of a type one error occurring.

The chi-square test

This measures whether the differences in cross tabulated data sets are significant. This is also known as 'goodness of fit' between observed distribution and expected distribution of the variable. It compares one or more sets of data to indicate if there is a real difference.

A chi-square test of two or more variables can be used to test, for example, the difference between male and female respondents to the mailing.

Hypotheses about means

Where sample data produces a mean or a proportion, researchers can use a Z or a T test to test hypotheses relating to them.

Z tests are used if the researcher is aware of the population's mean and variance. This may be the real mean or variance, or assumed figures. The sample must be higher than 30. T tests are used if the mean and variance are unknown or if a sample is less than 30. T tests are more frequently used by researchers. They allow the researcher to work out if the difference between the two averages is real or significant, or simply due to the fact that the figures are derived from a sample. For example, if a customer-satisfaction survey ranks your brand higher than average, is this a real difference or due to sampling error?

In a sample of 1500 people on a scale of 1–5 your customer satisfaction was 4.5, the average of your competitors was 3.8. The sample standard deviation was 1.6.

The formula for a Z test is as follows:

$$Z = \frac{\text{sample mean} - \text{population}}{\text{estimated standard error}}$$

Standard error = standard deviation/the square root of the sample size

$$\text{Standard error} = \frac{1.6}{\sqrt{1500}} = 0.04$$

$$Z = (4.5 - 3.8)/0.04 = 17.5$$

This is larger than the Z value of 1.64 at 0.05 level of significance and we can say that at 95 per cent confidence the results are correct.

Try changing some of these figures, the standard deviation for example. You will see that if the results were more dispersed, the Z score would reduce.

T tests are generally used to determine the results from smaller surveys with a sample size of under 30.

The formula for T tests involving a mean and one sample is:

$$T = \frac{\text{sample mean} - \text{mean under null hypotheseis}}{\text{estimated standard error of the mean}}$$

For comparing the mean in two samples the following formula is used:

$$T = \frac{\text{mean from sample 1} - \text{mean from sample 2}}{\sqrt{[(\text{standard error for sample 1})^2 - (\text{standard error for sample 2})^2}}$$

Measuring relationships

Correlation and regression

These techniques measure the degree of association between two variables such as income and number of foreign holidays or customer satisfaction and product repurchase, or advertising spend and sales.

Bivariate techniques measure the relationship between two variables. This does not prove that one variable causes the other but rather indicates the degree of relationship between the variables. Often a cause-and-effect link is assumed but this is not a proven relationship. It is important to apply common sense in the interpretation of the results.

Variables are labelled dependent and independent. Independent variables are those assumed to influence the dependent variable.

There are two types of correlation analysis.

Pearson's product movement correlation is used with interval and ratio data. It produces a correlation coefficient which can have a maximum value of +1 and a minimum value of −1.

Perfect positive correlation between two sets of variables is indicated by +1. This means that if there is a movement of 5 per cent on one variable, it is accompanied by a movement in the same direction of 5 per cent on another variable. For example, when satisfaction increases by 5 per cent, sales rise by 5 per cent. Perfect negative correlation means the two variables have a perfect negative relationship. If for every 10 per cent increase in price the sales volume decreased by 10 per cent, then the correlation coefficient would be −1.

When changes in one variable are not associated with changes in the other variable, the correlation coefficient will be calculated as zero.

Generally, correlation coefficients above +0.7 or below −0.7 are believed to show an increasing degree of association. This might require further research to explore the association in more detail from larger samples.

When ordinal data is being considered, **Spearman's rank order correlation** is used. This might be used to compare ranking of companies' promotional expenditure with a ranking of their sales turnover.

It is important to note that low coefficients do not mean that there is no association. It only implies absence of a linear association. It may be that a non-linear association exists. Again think about your market and apply common sense to your work.

Simple regression analysis

Regression analysis is concerned with dependence. For example, sales volume may be predicted based on other variables.

In the insurance industry, this is used to measure the chance of a customer not renewing a policy and explores the number of inbound calls and customer complaints.

The allocation of dependent and independent variables is more important in regression analysis. Remember, movement in the dependent variables depends upon movement in the independent variables.

Often, correlation analysis and regression analysis are both carried out on the same data sets. If correlation analysis indicates which variables have a relevant association with, say, sales volume, regression analysis can be used to predict sales volume, given a set of decisions about marketing variables and assumptions about probable movements in external variables. Sales forecasters use regression analysis. However, it is clear that the movement in a market is caused by a number of factors and this is dealt with through multivariate techniques which we will look at later.

Least squares is the most common approach to regression. Least squares identifies a line of best fit between observations and this allows us to produce an estimated regression function that indicates the relationship. To do this we need to look at the slope of the line and the line of intercept. Simple regression analysis may be enhanced through the coefficient of determination. This measures the strength of the relationship between variables.

Multivariate analysis techniques

These techniques analyse two or more variables simultaneously and present a more realistic approach to marketing decision-making.

There are six key techniques:

Multiple regression analysis

This allows the researcher to understand the relationship between three or more variables and the impact on the value of a dependent value, based on the values of two or more independent values – for example, response to mailings and the impact of re-mailing or telephone follow-up. Wilson points out that there are three common uses:

◆ The impact of marketing mix variables on sales

◆ The importance of components or aspects of satisfaction on overall satisfaction

◆ Determining the impact of different consumer characteristics on sales.

Multiple discriminant analysis

This technique is used to classify individuals based on two or more independent variables, for example, readiness to buy a car based on age of car, length of time spent on the website and in-bound calls.

The major discriminating factor between shoppers and non-shoppers in a particular department store was found, through discriminant analysis, to be the perceived price level within the store. Subsequent advertising of lower-priced lines resulted in an increase in the number of shoppers.

Factor analysis

Factor analysis reduces a large number of variables to a more manageable smaller set of factors based on the interrelationships between them. It provides insight for the groupings that emerge and allows for more efficient analysis of complex data. It is often used for rating scales or attitude statements.

Factor analysis is a subjective process as any set of factors can be rejected and new sets created. One way of managing this is to split the sample into two groups and if the same factors are created from each group, more confidence can be placed in them.

Cluster analysis

This technique groups objects or respondents into mutually exclusive and exhaustive groups. The technique is often used in database marketing to create segments based on behaviour across a range of variables.

Multidimensional scaling or perceptual mapping

Consumers rate objects, often brands, by the relative strength of an attribute compared to other objects or brands. This creates a perception of a 'position' in the market and is very useful for determining brand perception and repositioning.

Conjoint analysis

Conjoint analysis is a way of looking at customers' decisions as a trade-off between multiple attributes in products or services.

In conjoint analysis, consumers are asked to make decisions about various attributes, trading lower price for comfort, for example, in car purchases.

There are two approaches to this process:

1   The full-profile approach describes the full product or service – respondents may rank all possible combinations of, for example, product quality, price and after sales service.

2   The pairwise approach presents attributes in pairs and respondents put each in rank order. This approach is generally easier for respondents to manage and care must be taken that the list of attributes is not too long.

Software packages

There are many software packages on the market that will do most of this for you. The key thing is to understand what these packages will do to your valuable data and to produce efficient analysis which allows a focus on the research problem. Snap software will analyse questionnaires for you and Excel is perfectly adequate for most of the key formulae outlined above but there are specialists, perhaps the best known software package for analysis is SPSS (www.spss.com).

Presentation of the results

Once data has been analysed it is presented back to clients. Remember we covered the analysis of qualitative data in Unit 6. Now we are bring all our data together and producing a solution, meet the objectives set for the research study.

The final report to the client is perhaps the most important part of the research planning process. For the external agency, it is the moment of truth when the proposed methodology is presented to the client. For the client, it is the chance to consider the course of action based on the results. For individuals, it is the chance to impress senior colleagues and enhance their reputation. No wonder people get a little fractious and nervous as the deadline looms!

The ability to present data in the most appropriate and accessible way, whilst ensuring that the research problem is effectively dealt with, is a highly developed skill. The results are generally presented in written format and this may or may not be supported by an oral presentation supported by slides.

Wilson suggests a six-point approach to the presentation of research that focuses on the audience's needs.

1 Respect their importance

2 What do they need from the report

3 How does your report meet this need

4 Underpin the key information with evidence

5 Remind them of the key points of the report

6 Make recommendations as to action.

Let's look at each of these in a little more depth:

1 Respect their importance

The report should and presentation should be:

- Well presented
- To the point
- Clear
- Addresses objectives
- Well structured around the needs of the audience.

2 Consider their needs

- It must contain clear rationale and objectives
- It should be tailored to their knowledge levels
- It must be engaging and interesting.

3 Show how the research helps me

- It must link back to the objectives and focus on actions
- Results focused on core outcomes
- It must drive marketing decisions – insight not data.

4 Evidence must be presented persuasively

- Explain the detail
- Convince of accuracy
- Charts, tables and respondents' quotes
- Data on supporting CD
- Bring this to life, vox pops, video, mood boards
- Anticipate and pre-empt questions.

5 Remind of the key points

- Organise your material around a clear contents and agenda
- Recap and review

    ◆ Tell them what you are going to tell them, tell them, tell them what you have told them.

6   Advise them

    ◆ Clear concise recommendations are needed. What should I do as a result of this?

    ◆ Marketing and business recommendations.

The written report

Before producing the report, it helps to consider the objectives of the study again and the nature of the audience who will read and use the report.

◆   What are the key points that the audience is interested in?

◆   What are the key constraints on marketing decisions recommended in the report? What is the business position

◆   What are the resource implications of decisions adequately considered?

Research report format

The structure of a written report is standard and this helps considerably with the process of producing the document. A report would normally contain these elements, with variations to suit the nature of the research and house styles.

◆   **Title page** – all necessary information

◆   **Table of contents**

◆   **Headings** and subheadings

◆   **Executive summary** – one to three pages, completed after the report

◆   **Introduction**

◆   **Problem definition**

◆   **Proposal review**

◆   **Research method and limitations**

◆   **Research findings**

◆   **Conclusions and core recommendations**

◆   **Appendices**

Title page

This should contain the title of the report, the name and contact details of the agency and the researcher, client details and the date of presentation.

Table of contents

This should contain full details of sections, subsections and page numbers, and include lists of tables and figures. It should make the report navigable. If presenting on the Web, the use of hyperlinks which take the browser to the relevant section can be considered.

The executive summary

This should be a short summary of the report and its recommendations. Many say that it should be a one- or two-page summary, or a maximum of two pages. There are no hard and fast rules. The summary needs to do a job, that is, summarizing a report, and also needs to be accessible.

Production of the executive summary is a tough job. As Churchill said 'Sorry, for such a long letter. I didn't have time to write a short one.' It is hard to condense the report into a one- or two-page summary. It is also the section of the report that will be read by senior managers and so it is worth putting time and effort into its production.

The executive summary should be written after the rest of the report has been completed, but should start the report. Some people feel that it should follow the contents page and some feel that it should precede it. Some companies produce a separate summary of the work and this can be useful for wider and more efficient distribution of the findings.

Introduction

The introduction should outline the key objectives of the research, the reasons why the research has been carried out and the constraints that the researchers are working to. It may include profiles and key responsibilities of the researchers.

Situation analysis and problem definition

This section outlines the background to the problem and reviews business and marketing objectives. It drills down into the problem's definition and the detailed objectives for the research programme, and reprises the sections of the brief and proposal.

Research methodology and limitations

This section outlines the detailed methodology for the study. It should cover the research method, the data capture mechanism, the topic or discussion guide or questionnaire, the definition of the population of interest, the sampling approach and the method of data analysis. This section should not be too long. Details should be put into the appendices. It should cover sources of error, including sample size.

Findings and analysis

The main body of the report should cover the findings relevant to the objectives. It should be constructed to present a solution to the problem, not on a question-by-question basis. The research data should present data to support a line of argument and the focus should be on analysis and insight. Key ideas can be supported by tables or quotes from respondents. It may include tables and graphics, and should be linked by a narrative.

Conclusions and recommendations

This section brings the report to a close. It should present a summary of key findings and recommendations for marketing decisions and future research.

Appendices

Should include all supporting data. It contains material that is relevant to the research but that would be too detailed for the main report. It may include all tables, questionnaires, discussion guides and secondary data. It may be that the appendices are longer than the main report.

Example of a report contents (amended to protect client confidentiality)

1   Executive summary

2   Acknowledgements

3   Introduction

    (a) Industry background – The UK market

        i.   The 'Brand Renaissance'

        ii.   A radically changing distribution network

        iii. Changing consumer values

        iv.   The franchised dealer

    (b) Background to organization

        i.   UK success story?

        ii.   Brand deficit

        iii. The future

4   Research objectives

5   Research methodology

    (a) Sampling procedure and size

    (b) Research methods

        i.   In-depth interviews

        ii.   Staff focus groups

        iii. Customer focus groups

6   Data analysis and evaluation

7   Research findings

    (a) Primary research overview

    (b) Strategic direction of the brand

    (c) Staff perception of the brand

    (d) Staff and customer value

    (e) Loyalty and interaction of staff

    (f) Effective communication

    (g) Measurement as a behavioural driver

    (h) Customer value of experience

    (i) Brand decision-making

8   Conculsions

9   Appendices

    (a) Appendix A: In-depth interview guide

    (b) Appendix B: Staff focus group discussion guide

    (c) Appendix C: Customer focus group discussion guide

    (d) Appendix D: Participant invitation letter

    (e) Appendix E: CD Rom recording of in-depth interviews

    (f) Appendix F: Video footage of focus groups

10   Terms of reference.

The layout of the formal written report should conform to house style. Generally, companies that are producing a large number of reports will include the format of the report in their identity guidelines or will have formal guidelines elsewhere that should be followed. The font size and appearance must do justice to your work and the sequencing of the report with its headers and subheaders should make the report more accessible.

A style guide might also be used to help with language, grammar and even brand messages through the report. If you are unsure of English, then it is always best to get somebody professional to proofread your work for spelling, grammar and punctuation. Remember that proofreading is different from reading the report through. Each word and sentence needs to be considered individually as well as in connection with the rest of the report.

The oral presentation

Delivering an oral presentation may be daunting, but preparation means that it does not have to be too nerve-wracking. In many cases nerves are a good sign that this matters.

The oral presentation may involve a number of people and a range of audio and visual equipment. The technology is always a problem and it is reassuring to have a back-up.

The key thing in preparing a presentation is that it is not simply a regurgitation of the report. It will, of course, draw on the same data and make the same conclusions but the findings can be presented in a much livelier and, maybe, accessible and memorable way.

Wilson (2006) presents a useful structure for research presentations:

Introduction

- Thank you.
- Introduce the team.
- Outline the agenda of the presentation.
- Set rules for questions. Will you take them at the end or through the presentation?

Research background and objectives

An outline of the business and marketing background and the objectives of the study.

Research methodology

Describe the methodology and data collection device along with limitations.

Key findings

Supported by graphs and tables. Keep it simple, only present pertinent tables and graphs. Make sure that the tables and graphs are readable and clear.

Conclusions and recommendations

Repeat key findings. Lay down your recommendations.

Questions

A full discussion of the issues. Think about the following points at rehearsal:

1 What questions will come up? Try to pre-empt and prepare.

2 Will all presenters handle questions or will the team leader take questions and pass them on to the team's expert?

3 What will you do if you cannot answer a question?

4 Tell your audience how you want to deal with questions.

Presentation tips

◆ Meet your objectives. State them early on and show throughout how your presentation contributes to their achievement. You might even ask the audience what their objectives are at the beginning of the presentation, note them on a flip chart and at the end of the presentation tick them off.

◆ Know your audience; what do they want to hear? How many will be present? Who are they? What positions do they hold?

◆ How will you dress? Is it formal or informal or will you be overdressed in a suit and a tie? What do your audience expect?

◆ Keep it brief and to the point, do not use too many tables and graphs. Use a balanced mixture of words and images. Keep to time.

◆ Be prepared for interruptions and stop presenting if your audience are distracted. Do not plough on.

◆ Turn off mobile phones and ask your audience to do the same. Try to manage the physical characteristics of the room, heat and lighting, and air conditioning.

◆ If using PowerPoint technology, make sure that it is compatible with the projection system. Make sure that your slides do not contain too much information and that tables and graphics can be read.

◆ During the presentation, maintain eye contact with your audience. Try to avoid having a physical barrier between you and your audience.

◆ Be aware of your body language, relax your shoulders, smile and try to project enthusiasm.

◆ Relax and use natural movements. Engage with your audience but do not invade their personal space.

◆ Make eye contact with all people in the room early on – get them on your side.

◆ Face your audience rather than the screen. If you are able to, determine where each member of the team presenting and the audience will sit.

◆ Never turn your back to the audience.

◆ Do not hide behind lecterns and A4 notes.

◆ Use cue cards if necessary, do not try to ad lib unless you are well rehearsed.

◆ Provide handouts for your audience of the slides, tables and graphs that may be hard to read.

◆ If working with a team of presenters, make sure that you support them. When you are not presenting, maintain a positive attitude and listen to the rest of the team. If a team member falters or technology is causing problems, act to sort out the situation. Do not sit there thinking thank goodness that is not me. You will be judged by the performance of the team as a whole.

◆ Keep to time and take responsibility for your own timings. Some audiences for competitive pitches will stop a presentation if it overruns.

◆ Use pictures, video and audio clips to enliven and add variety to the presentation, but do not make a presentation over busy.

Research has shown that people forget 30 per cent of what they are told after just three hours and 90 per cent after only three days. Visual aids can help and variety is the key. The combination of verbal and visual material has been shown to deliver 85 per cent recollection after three hours and up to 65 per cent after three days.

Almost all presentations are made using PowerPoint and the lack of pacing and variety often creates a very flat atmosphere and passive audience. This is often the case as projection equipment may mean that the lights have to be dimmed and the audience sink into a soporific state. Popcorn might be a more appropriate snack than the executive biscuit selection. Liven it up by using a variety of support and dynamic pacing through the presentation.

   ◆ Flipchart
   ◆ Overhead projector slides
   ◆ PowerPoint
   ◆ Story boards
   ◆ Video and sound clips.

◆ Practise, practise, practise, remember 'fail to prepare, prepare to fail'.

   ◆ Make sure you carry out a 'dress' rehearsal. Practise speaking out loud.
   ◆ Practise all aspects of the presentation including the transition between speakers and the use of supporting technology or audio-visual aids.
   ◆ It may help to record your rehearsal and pick up your verbal tics, the 'you knows' the 'hums' and the 'yeses'. Knowing that you have these verbal tics can help control them. Practise volume and pace and the use of silence.

◆ Tell them what you will tell them, tell them and tell them what you have told them. Structure the presentation and use staging posts and summarizing slides to close sections and introduce new sections.

◆ Always start and finish on a high note.

◆ Do not be shy about saying that you want the business.

Use of graphics

Tables and graphs will enliven reports and presentations, but with the range of technology available, overkill is possible.

Tables

Tables should be presented with the title and a number. The tables should be labelled with base numbers, that is, the figures for the sample and subsamples should be shown, especially when percentages are being used. 75 per cent is impressive. 75 per cent of 10 respondents is less so. If quantities are indicated in the table, you must specify if they are in volumes or value. If numbers are used, specify the units. If currency is used, make sure that it is included in the table description.

Tables should be structured so that data is ordered from large to small items. The layout should enable data to be read easily. If data is imported, it should always be referenced or sourced. Tables should, if appropriate, contain totals and subtotals. Numbers should be right justified. You should normally work to two decimal places.

| | Total | Gender | | Age | | | | |
		Male	Female	Under 18	18-24	25-44	45-60	Over 60
Total	**204**	**108**	**96**	**59**	**40**	**41**	**44**	**20**
Speed of service								
Very Good	52 25%	20 19%	32 33%	24 41%	16 40%	4 10%	4 9%	4 20%
Good	96 47%	56 52%	40 42%	27 46%	20 50%	25 61%	20 45%	4 20%
OK	40 20%	28 26%	12 13%	8 14%	4 10%	8 20%	16 36%	4 20%
Poor	12 6%	4 4%	8 8%	- -	- -	4 10%	4 9%	4 20%
Very Poor	4 2%	- -	4 4%	- -	- -	- -	- -	4 20%
Mean	0.88	0.85	0.92	1.27	1.30	0.71	0.55	0.00
Standard Error	0.06	0.07	0.11	0.09	0.10	0.12	0.12	0.32
Significance	0.00	0.50	0.50	0.98	0.97	0.63	0.92	1.00

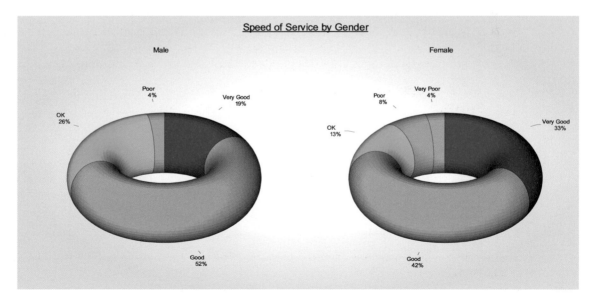

Figure 10.3: Snap generated tables and graphics

Source: reproduced with permission www.snapsurveys.com

Other graphics

Other graphical devices that can be used include:

Pie charts

Courses taken

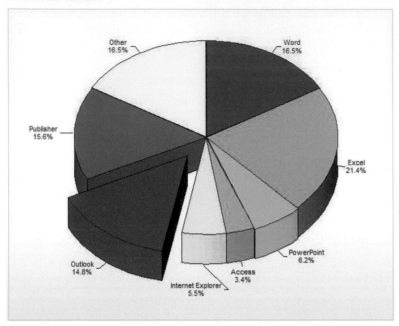

Figure 10.4: Pie charts

Bar charts
Students by age and gender

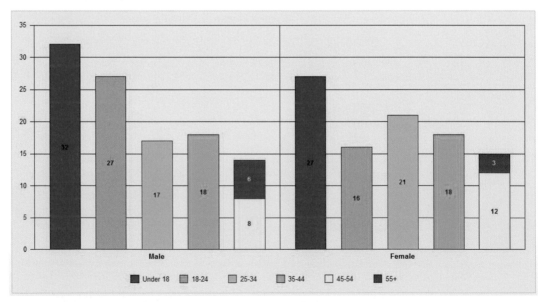

Figure 10.5: bar charts

Source: reproduced with permission www.snapsurveys.com

Excel charts and graphs

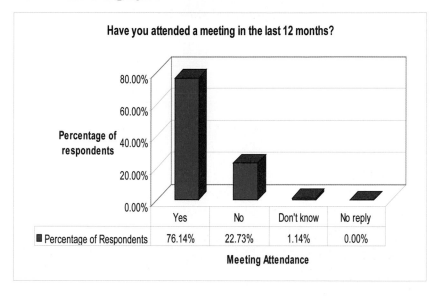

Figure 10.6: Bar chart created in Excel

Figure 10.7: Line graph created in Excel

Pictograms

These are graphics that are illustrated with pictures representing the product or object of the graphic. In a survey on beer consumption, for example, it might be illustrated by beer glasses of varying sizes.

PowerPoint slides

The ubiquity of PowerPoint means that often presentations can look very similar. So how will you make yours stand out? The role of a good corporate identity is important here. Equally it is tempting to overdress PowerPoint slides. Keep it simple; laying down text on 'watermarks' may reduce comprehension. Minimum font size should be 24 to ensure good legibility.

Problems in presentations

Wilson (2006) presents a list of common problems in presenting reports:

◆ Assuming understanding – there is insufficient background and interpretation given to results.

◆ Excessive length.

◆ Unrealistic recommendations which are commercially naive.

◆ Spurious accuracy – results are based on too-small sample sizes.

◆ Obscure statistics – a range of obscure techniques may not be useful if the client cannot use them.

◆ Over-elaborate presentation – too many graphics and presentational devices may obscure more than it reveals.

Summary

In this unit, we looked at the process of data analysis and presentation. We saw that data needs to be entered, coded, edited and cleaned before data analysis can be carried out.

We saw that there are four types of data. These are:

◆ Nominal

◆ Ordinal

◆ Interval

◆ Ratio.

The type of analysis that can be carried out is dependent on the type of data that is being analysed.

We looked at the process of tabulation. In order to obtain a first look at data, we saw examples of frequency distributions or hole counts and cross tabulation.

We went on to look at the types of analysis that can be carried out looking in detail at the following:

◆ Descriptive statistics

◆ Statistical significance and hypotheses testing

◆ The measurement of relationships

◆ Multivariate analysis.

We looked in detail at methods under each of these categories.

We went on to look at the process of delivering results from research.

We looked at the structure of a written research report and covered each of these sections in depth:

◆ Title page

- Contents
- Executive summary
- Introduction
- Situation analysis and problem definition
- Research methodology and limitations
- Findings and analysis
- Conclusions and recommendations
- Appendices.

We went on to cover the oral presentation of the results and gave tips for presentation success

- Introduction
- Research background and objectives
- Research methodology
- Key findings
- Conclusions and recommendations
- Questions.

We then looked at the graphical presentation of the results including:

- Tables
- Bar graphs
- Pie charts and donuts
- Line graphs
- Pictograms.

Finally, we looked at common failings in presenting results.

Bibliography

Wilson, A. (2006) *Marketing Research: An Integrated Approach*, FT Prentice Hall, 2nd edition

Website

www.snapsurveys.com

Appendix

Feedback and answers

Unit 1

Activity 1.1

The CIM definition

You should have written

The management process responsible for identifying, anticipating and satisfying customer requirements profitably. (CIM 2008)

Activity 1.2

You probably have a long list which might include the following:

♦ I am thirsty.
♦ I am hot.
♦ I am concerned about the chemical contents of tap water.
♦ I care for my family.
♦ I want a healthy lifestyle.
♦ I am buying packaged water for convenience.
♦ I am going to the gym and need to rehydrate.
♦ I like sparkling water with my meal.
♦ Buying this water says that I am sophisticated.
♦ I like the taste of this brand.
♦ I like the new packaging.
♦ It is cheaper than cola.
♦ I make a better margin on this brand of water.
♦ My staff enjoy discussing business around the water cooler.

Activity 1.3

You may have listed some or all of the following. The list is not exhaustive if you have other organizations listed use the definition to decide if they are genuine stakeholders.

♦ Suppliers
♦ Competitors
♦ Distributors
♦ Shareholders
♦ Policy-makers
♦ Regulators
♦ Government agencies
♦ Retailers and other intermediaries
♦ Customers
♦ Unions
♦ Pressure groups
♦ Pensioners
♦ Local community
♦ Investors.

Activity 1.4

You may have a list that includes some or all of the following factors:

Political considerations, highlights the role of government at national and regional and level

♦ Government stability
♦ Type of government
♦ Taxation policy
♦ Welfare policy
♦ Foreign trade regulations
♦ Social welfare policies

Economic considerations, refers to macro economic factors

♦ GDP/GNP
♦ Disposable income
♦ International trade levels and tariffs
♦ National competitive advantage
♦ Money supply
♦ Interest rates
♦ Disposable incomes
♦ Welfare entitlements
♦ Unemployment
♦ Inflation

- Recession/Depression
- Exchange rates
- Interest rates
- State of stock markets
- Tax rates
- Savings incentives
- Economic systems

Socio-cultural considerations, changing culture and demographics

- Population demographics
- Gender, age, ethnicity, race, religion, working age population
- Income distribution
- Social mobility and stratification
- Lifestyle changes
- Attitudes to work and leisure
- Consumerism
- Levels of education and training
- Social change and changing social attitude

Technological considerations, the role of innovations and technical change

- Government spending on research
- Government and industry focus on technological effort
- New discoveries /developments
- Speed of technology transfer
- Rates of obsolescence
- Levels of research and development
- Subsidies for research and development
- Environmental considerations, the role of green issues
- Waste disposal
- Energy consumption
- Impact of fossil fuels
- Raw material resource depletion
- Air and soil contamination
- Protection of the environment
- Conservation
- Recycling
- Alternative forms of energy

Legal considerations, legislative constraints and changes

- Competition law
- Employment law

- Health and safety
- Product safety
- Environmental protection laws
- Business ownership laws
- Company law
- Disclosure laws
- Planning and property law

Activity 1.5

You may have covered some or all of the following:

- Employee knowledge and competencies, for example the sales force, call centre staff and so on
- Experiential knowledge at individual and group level, for example work with other companies on other projects
- Informal shared knowledge, the internal beliefs and values that sustain a business
- Task-based knowledge, as a result of certain functional specialisms or activity
- Knowledge from the database, for example accounts, operations, logistics, etc.
- Knowledge from internal structures, for example intranets, the relationship between departments and internal suppliers
- Knowledge from external structures, for example extranets, supplier and intermediary relationships
- Knowledge of customers through all touch points, for example research, Internet analysis, customer databases, CRM systems, sales force, contact centres, etc.

Unit 2

Activity 2.1

You probably have a few points of similarity and they may include the following:

- The database may be manual or computerized, but, almost always, today it will be computerized.
- It is a source of accurate up-to-date information or data about our past, present and current customers.
- It is relevant to the organization's goals.
- Data is collected systematically.
- Data is maintained and monitored.
- It is used to formulate strategy.
- It supports the formulation of marketing objectives of the enterprise.

Activity 2.2

So, what do you have? Below are some of the data elements you might have written down. We'll start with consumer markets:

Consumer identification data

♦ Customer reference number
♦ First name
♦ Last name
♦ Title – Mr, Mrs, Dr and so on
♦ Suffixes, for example B.A., M.A., Ph.D., M.CIM. and so on
♦ Date of birth
♦ Address
♦ Postcode
♦ Telephone
♦ E-mail
♦ Sales area
♦ Media sales area
♦ Fax
♦ Account number.

Demographic data

♦ Gender
♦ Age
♦ Occupation
♦ Employment status
♦ Marital status
♦ How many children?
♦ What age are the children?
♦ Financial
♦ Job title
♦ Income
♦ What is their credit history and rating?
♦ Are they a homeowner?
♦ What is the value of their home?
♦ Do they own a car?
♦ Share ownership
♦ Do they have a credit card?
♦ What insurance products do they have?

Lifestyle

♦ Life stage – student, retired and so on
♦ Number of holidays per year

- Where do they holiday?
- What leisure interests do they have?
- Media reading
- TV viewing.

Shopping behaviour

- When did they last buy? – Recency
- How often do they buy? – Frequency
- What is the value of their purchases? – Value
- What profit does the customer generate for the business over time? – Lifetime value
- Loyalty scheme member.

Other

- Length of time at current address
- Have they responded before?
- To what campaign?
- Customer service history
- Complaints
- Are they a VIP?
- Data protection issues
- Have they opted out of or into communications?
- Are they a shareholder?

Now let's look at business data:

Business data is often more complex to collect due to the nature of the business decision making process. There is generally more than one person in the decision-making unit and there maybe multiple locations to consider.

Business identification data

- Company name
- Trading name
- Trading status
- Credit rating
- Contact name or names in the decision-making unit
- Job title
- Areas of responsibility
- Address
- Website address
- Postcode
- Key contact
- Contact name
- Job
- Telephone
- Fax

- E-mail
- Account number
- VAT number
- Region
- Territory
- Salesperson.

Business details

- Size of business
- Turnover
- Employees
- Number of offices
- Head office
- Budget
- Financial year end.

Transaction data

- Account number
- Purchase history
- Recency, frequency and value
- Order size
- Service history
- Response
- Method of acquisition.

Sector

- Standard Industrial Classification code (SIC)
- Type of business.

Activity 2.4

You may have covered some or all of the following and may have others. Any contact between the organisation and its customers is capable of generating data.

- Sales
- Warranty registrations
- Enquiries/help line
- Complaints
- Sales Promotions
- Prize draws
- Competitions
- Coupon redemptions
- Marketing research & surveys, with due attention to data protection
- Accounts
- Third parties & marketing partners

♦ Branches & channels
♦ Servicing
♦ Direct response to communications
♦ PR events

Unit 3

Activity 3.3

Quite a few things to consider - aren't there.

Amongst others you may have:

♦ Is there a market for whisky-based drinks?
♦ What is the market worth?
♦ Who is the target market?
♦ What are their characteristics?
♦ What is the reaction of the retail and catering trade?
♦ How will the competition react?
♦ What brand strategy should we pursue?
♦ What shall we call the product?
♦ How much will it cost to produce?
♦ What price should we charge?

How should we promote the product? and so on. The list is long.

Unit 6

Activity 6.1

Your discussion guide should follow a similar structure to the example on page 110. You may have not been quite as precise with the timings for the various activities.

Activity 6.2

Volvo is interesting; despite the millions spent in advertising Volvo as an exciting car to drive, non-Volvo drivers will invariably describe the Volvo as:

Male

Middle class

Married with children (2.5)

Two black Labradors and a pair of green wellies.

While Volvo owners may present a different view this tends to be the perception of non-Volvo drivers.

Unit 9

Activity 9.2

- Are you single?
  (A sensitive question; ask the respondent to state what their marital status is.)

- What is your average weekly disposable income?
  (A sensitive question and hard for respondents to work out.)

- How regularly do you come here?
  (Ambiguous. Once a year or once a week.)

- Do you buy green vegetables?
  (Cabbage, fair trade or organics?)

- Do you by frozen and canned foods?
  (Spelling is poor, and there are two questions in one.)

- What about our chilled and ambient ready meals?
  (Two questions in one, and what are ambient ready meals? Will the respondent understand the question?)

- How much did you spend on food last year?
  (Can you remember this?)

- Most people say our new store layout is really good. What do you think?
  (A leading and loaded question.)

- Does your husband come with you?
  (Assumption about marital status, and unnecessary given the opening question.)

- When do you leave the car?
  (Assumption and 'when' does the researcher mean? – Overnight? When we go on holiday?)

- Are you against drug abuse?
  (A leading question, this would not produce a varied response.)

- You don't think council tax is too high, do you?
  (Use of negative and a leading question.)

- If we moved to the high street would you come more often?
  (A hypothetical question.)

- How old are your children?
  > 0–3
  > 3–5
  > 5–10
  > 10–15
  > 15+

  (Overlapping categories and what about parents of grown-up children?)

Index